*This book is dedicated to the
memory of my friend and brother-
in-law
the late Bob Shimer (1943-2004.)
He was a part of my life for
over forty years. In that time, he
brought me a lot of laughter, joy,
and love.
I miss him dearly.*

I Think I'm Having One Of Those Decades

By
Gordon Kirkland

Bloomington, IN  Milton Keynes, UK

authorHOUSE®

AuthorHouse™
1663 Liberty Drive, Suite 200
Bloomington, IN 47403
www.authorhouse.com
Phone: 1-800-839-8640

AuthorHouse™ UK Ltd.
500 Avebury Boulevard
Central Milton Keynes, MK9 2BE
www.authorhouse.co.uk
Phone: 08001974150

First published by AuthorHouse 7/5/2006

ISBN: 1-4259-1405-5 (sc)

Library of Congress Control Number: 2006900572

Printed in the United States of America
Bloomington, Indiana

This book is printed on acid-free paper.

Also By Gordon Kirkland

Books

Justice Is Blind – And Her Dog Just Peed In My Cornflakes

Never Stand Behind A Loaded Horse

When My Mind Wanders It Brings Back Souvenirs

Compact Disks

Comedy

I'm Big For My Age

Audiobooks

Never Stand Behind A Loaded Horse – Live

The Gordon Kirkland Writer To Writer Series Compact Disks

Live At The Florida First Coast Writers' Festival – Write For Your Life

Writing Humor – Even On Days When You Don't Feel Funny

Table of Contents

Acknowledgements

My wife Diane takes credit for my career as a writer. The thing is, she's right. Without her support, I wouldn't be able to have had the success that I've enjoyed over the past decade.

I've also had a decade's worth of support from our two sons, Mike and Brad, who seem to have survived spending their teen years as characters in my columns. It couldn't have been too hard on them because we've had to install a revolving door on our rarely empty nest.

You'll note that this book is dedicated to the memory of Bob Shimer, by brother-in-law who passed away in December of 2004. He was a great friend and supporter. My sister, Lois, my brother, Jim, and I were lucky to have him in our lives, and I am blessed to have the two of them in my corner.

Roy Sullivan has been one of my closest friends for over thirty years. He knows how important he is to me, and now so do the rest of you. Everyone needs a friend you can duel with in the middle of a Toronto street with shaken champagne bottles at ten paces.

One of the greatest pleasures I've had over the past few years is meeting other writers at the writers' conferences I've spoken at throughout North America. Each year I make thirty days available in my touring schedule for these events, as my way of 'paying it forward' to the people who helped me get my start in the business.

Of these, I want to make special mention of the Erma Bombeck Writers' Workshop at the University of Dayton and its Director, Tim Bete. Being asked to join the faculty of that workshop gave me a huge boost in my profile as a writer. Having the opportunity to work with Tim, a very funny writer in his own right, as well as with the attendees and other faculty members, has been a great joy. Quite frankly, the workshop is too much fun to be legal in certain states.

It has also given me the chance to meet and share laughter with Erma's widower Bill, their daughter Betsy, and sons Andrew and Matt. It also allowed me to thank them for sharing their mother through her column, which blazed the trail for the rest of us in this business.

In addition, I'd like to acknowledge the folks at AuthorHouse™ who have been so great to work with over the past couple of years. Bryan Smith, Matt Patton, Brad Collins, Kelly Barrow (the world's greatest cover designer), Kelli Shute, Erica Dorocke, Trina Lee, Eric Bilinski, and so many others proved that making a book successful really is a team effort - and for a whole lot of fun in taverns, even if I did have to promise not to write about that one in New York City.

Thanks too, to Dave Barry, Ridley Pearson, Lynn Johnston, Bruce Cameron, and so many other writers who have helped and befriended me along the way and who share this insane life as fulltime writers.

Sylvia Taylor has had the thankless job of trying to edit my writing for this book, something she should probably be sainted for agreeing to do. Anyone willing to take on my dangling participles will probably end up discussing it with a therapist at some future date.

Friends and family make living this life worthwhile. To all of you who are reading this section to see if you got mentioned, consider it done. You know who you are and what you mean to me.

Of course, what's really important is to thank the readers who share my life and times and who view them through my eyes.

Introduction: I Think I'm Having One Of Those Decades

Have you ever had one of those decades?

I've had five of them and now I'm working on my sixth. I'm not sure if I'm ready to be fifty-two. I think you'd have to be a whole lot more grown up to be fifty two.

Ask anyone. I haven't come close to being grown up, and there really aren't any indications on the horizon that it's going to happen any time soon.

People like me do whatever is possible to avoid growing up.

Still, there are signs out there that everyone eventually has to grow up. They slow down, or stop to spend more time with their family, smell the roses, or take a laxative.

The fact that now qualify for membership in AARP is just downright scary. It just doesn't make sense. But then a lot of things don't make sense to me that I would have thought a person of fifty-two should understand.

- Quantum Physics
- How stuff stays in a compact disk
- Reality TV
- The need for fiber in the diet
- My sons being older than I was when I got married

There are other things that various members of my family and most - OK all - of my friends don't seem to understand. Most of them can be summed up with one of the two following statements:

- "He's fifty-two and he still acts like that?"
- "He's been married for thirty-two years and she still puts up with him acting like that?"

OK, I'm an enigma, but as Dave Barry says on the cover of this book, it beats having to go out and find a real job.

It's been an interesting decade for someone like me. Ten years ago, I had just started writing my newspaper column, so the whole decade has been focused on writing columns, magazine articles and books.

For all those people who can't believe that I could ever write a book—especially Miss Witherspoon, my eighth-grade English composition teacher, this is number four. On top of that, there have been over five hundred columns with my byline in newspapers in Canada and the United States since I started a decade and a bit ago.

Perhaps the best part of the decade has been the opportunities to meet the people who have been reading my work. I've done live, radio and television appearances in six Canadian provinces and twenty-three American states.

It's also been a decade that has shown me that there is life after a significant injury. I'm what is called an incomplete paraplegic. My wife, the long suffering Diane, says that it's just like any man; I never finish anything I start.

When I started writing these short bits of comedy in the Nineties, I didn't know if it was going to become a career. Now, over eleven years later, I've gained a certain amount of success and it looks as though, just like Mary Richards on the old Mary Tyler Moore Show, I just might make it after all.

I just don't think I can jump up and toss my hat the way she did.

So here is another collection of the stories that have made this one of those decades. I hope you enjoy reading them as much as I've enjoyed experiencing them.

Section 1
My Life Keeps Getting Stranger

Love Means Never Having To Say, "I'm Stuck In Traffic"

I've been married for over thirty-two years, which truly amazes most of our friends, family, and anyone who has ever read anything I've written. Diane is often questioned about how she has managed to put up with me for so long.

A while back, the alumni of the Erma Bombeck Writer's Workshop decided to create the Diane Kirkland Award, to be presented annually to the spouse of a humor writer who has had to put up with the most grief over the years. Diane was the first recipient.

When my friend Lynn Johnston, the creator of the *For Better Or For Worse* comic strip, wrote the cover comments for my second book, she said, *"Nothing is safe from his crack-the-wit columns, which is why I love to read his stuff . . . I just wouldn't want to be married to him!"*

Somehow - and I can't imagine where it comes from - people have gotten the idea that it would be difficult to put up with someone like me for three decades and change.

I'd like to set the record straight. In fact, ladies and gentlemen, I'm an absolute freaking saint. As a result of my pure, unadulterated saintliness, Diane and I share an abiding love that has sustained us through the years.

They say that opposites attract, and I will admit that in many ways Diane and I are opposites. One only needs to look at the two of us to see a myriad of differences.

I'm six-foot-four and Diane is nearly a foot shorter. To make her feel better about her vertical deficiencies, I've always tried to keep the difference somewhat muted by saying that I too am five-foot-something. OK, so it's five-foot-sixteen, but at least I'm trying to stay within the same range.

If anything, our height difference has always worked to Diane's advantage. If she didn't have me around she would have to use an extension ladder to get anything from the top shelves in the kitchen cupboards.

Another difference is apparent because I've lost a great deal of the pigmentation in my hair. It seems to have accelerated considerably over the last few years. Diane is often quick to point out that she still has the same hair color she had when we were married, without the need to use artificial coloring. I'm happy to let her have that more youthful image and will regularly point it out, as well.

"Just look at Diane's hair color," I will often say. "Even though she's older than I am, it's still nice and dark. I guess that just goes to show which one of us is easier to live with, even if she does look younger then me."

See? That was just filled with compliments about her dark hair despite being my elder.

Like I said, I'm just a freaking saint.

After more than thirty years of marriage, people should accept that there is something special between us. With divorce rates as high as they are, it's almost becoming unusual for a couple to be together for so long. I think one recent event epitomizes what we have.

Diane is a stockbroker. In her business, the months of January and February are the busiest. As a result, she is working six days a week and several evenings as well. We don't get to see that much of each other in these two months. Diane asked me if I would like to go with her last Friday, when she needed to go downtown for a brief appointment.

Naturally, I thought that she was missing me during her busy season, and aware that I would be starting my appearance tour in just a couple of days. It warmed my heart to think she wanted to get a couple of extra hours of time together.

"Sure," I said, ever the freaking saint that I am. "I'll reschedule my day so we can have that time together."

She turned and said, "I'm so glad you'll come with me. That way I can use the carpool lane on the freeway."

If that's not love, I just don't know what it is.

"Aargh...Gord..."

I spent a recent morning in very familiar surroundings. Thirty-two years had passed since I couldn't wait to get out of the place, and yet, I found myself looking forward to the opportunity to re-enter the hallowed halls of good old Oakridge Secondary School in London, Ontario.

Go Oaks!

One of the things I really enjoy doing while I'm on tour is visiting, schools and talking to the students about the career opportunities an interest in writing can open up for them. Since I was making a tour stop in the city where I had spent my high school years, it seemed only right that I give my old school a call and offer to drop by for a visit.

OK. Maybe there were a few reasons against it, but you'd think that they would have forgotten about them in the years that have transpired since 1972, when I left high school behind for greater pursuits.

I survived high school by being the guy people turned to for a laugh. If I couldn't find anything funny going on, I took it as my solemn duty to provide something. As a result I knew the shortest route to the vice-principal's office from just about anywhere on the school property.

As class clowns go, I guess I was pretty lucky. Our vice-principal had a pretty good sense of humor in his own right. Still, I'm sure I tested his patience on a regular basis.

He would come on the intercom and just say, "Aargh, Gord...."

There could have been ten or twenty Gords going to that school, but everyone knew exactly which one he was talking about.

On one memorable occasion, my English class was putting on the play Romanoff and Juliet by Peter Ustinov. It was the story of the son of a Russian ambassador who had fallen in love with the daughter of the American ambassador, in a small European duchy at the height of the Cold War. I played the Russian ambassador.

There was a scene in which I was supposed to berate my chief spy for reading decadent American magazines. I decided to add a little laughter to our dress rehearsal by rigging a Playboy magazine so that when I picked it up saying the words "decadent American magazines" the centerfold would open, displaying its subject in all her glory.

And, as I recall, she had a lot of glory to display.

When you are on stage under the bright lights, and the house lights in the theater are turned out, you can't see anything past the edge of the stage. Unbeknownst to me, the elected officials on the school board had been invited to watch our dress rehearsal.

Within minutes, the intercom crackled to life and the words "Aargh... Gord..." echoed through the halls.

After my recent speech at Oakridge, one of the students in attendance presented me with a gift, representative of a moment in the school's history that has become legendary.

It was a large box of Ivory Snow™ laundry detergent.

On the last day of my senior year, a ten-pound box of Ivory Snow™ somehow made its way into the school fountain. The fountain was in a courtyard that was two classrooms wide by three classrooms long by two stories tall. It was designed to add more water automatically as needed, so the soap grew into a massive cloud that filled the courtyard completely. Soap suds drifted out over the roof and onto the busy street in front of the school.

I can remember seeing the janitor standing at a window quietly repeating, "Oh! Wow..."

As I left the school for the last time a few minutes later, I looked back at the building. The foam made it look like it had contracted rabies.

I left with the full knowledge of just how the soap had made its way into the fountain. A good number of the students also had a pretty good idea where it had come from, too.

One thing that I'm sure of, is that my dear old friend, the vice-principal, knew better than anyone just how the soap got there.

Oh, yes. He knew.

Though I had already left the building, I'd like to think that for old time's sake, he got on the intercom one last time and said the words I can still hear clearly in my mind today.

"Aargh...Gord..."

While One Curse Dies, Others Live On

The Curse of the Bambino may be gone, but the Curse of the Dadino lives on. It's doubtful that it will ever be broken.

I've never been a stellar athlete. My trophy collection includes a hockey championship trophy from 1964-65, and a golf trophy for being the most cost efficient golfer (I had the lowest cost per stroke) in a tournament in the Eighties.

Baseball, in our little town north of Toronto, was something you did to pass the time between hockey seasons. We had a bat, a glove, and several balls around the house, and they got a bit of use each summer.

In the summer of 1962, someone in the town got the idea that the local kids needed a little league to keep them occupied in the springtime. I thought it sounded like a good idea.

About thirty kids showed up at the baseball diamond in the schoolyard for the first night of organized little league baseball. The fathers who had agreed to act as coaches took turns hitting the ball out to the kids in the field. Eventually, it was my turn to be on the receiving end.

I didn't really realize what that would entail.

Somebody's dad hit a high pop fly towards me. I watched in awe as it flew up, up, up, and then disappeared as it reached its summit directly in front of the sun. I stood dumfounded in the field wondering where the ball had gone. I didn't need to wonder for too long. It reappeared on its downward slope a few feet from my forehead. I may have closed my eyes just before it hit.

They were definitely closed immediately after it hit.

If this was what organized baseball was all about, I wasn't sure if I wanted any part of it. Naturally, my father gave me the tried and true speech about the best thing to do when you fall off a horse, is to get right back up on it.

I hadn't fallen off a horse, and I told him that if he wanted to get me a horse, I would gladly get back on it whenever I fell off it. At least that wasn't going to involve intercontinental ballistic baseballs targeting my forehead.

I agreed that I would probably be safer the next week, because it was going to be batting practice, with the coaches slowly pitching the balls to us. I swung my bat mightily at each and every pitch.

Swinging the bat was not a problem. Hitting the ball with it was the problem.

The following Saturday, my father took me into the back yard to help me combine swinging the bat and hitting the ball. He pitched me a lovely slow ball. I could see it coming.

I swung, and heard that satisfying crack as the bat and the ball connected. Before my father could say anything there was another crack. Actually, it was more of a crash, followed by a whole bunch of tinkles. The ball had sailed through the master bedroom window.

The closed master bedroom window.

Batting practice was suspended, while my father went to the hardware store, bought a pane of glass and replaced the window.

When that was done, he took me back into the yard and told me he would show me how to aim the ball where I wanted it to go.

I threw the ball, and he swung. Once again there was the crash followed by a series of tinkles as the ball sailed through the just replaced master bedroom window.

That's when I heard the Curse of the Dadino. My father had a collection of curses that he used on a regular basis, and another that he brought out for special occasions.

This was clearly a special occasion. He used just about everything in his entire repertoire, some that I had not heard before or since. If trying to hit a ball with a bat meant getting knocked out, and watching while your father has his own personal nuclear meltdown, then that particular horse was not one I was willing to get back up on.

I still don't know how to aim a baseball, but hey, I'm not alone. Neither do the Seattle Mariners.

My, What A Lovely Gun You Have Pointed At Me

I guess it's a sign of the times we are living in, but it seems that police officers are a bit more nervous than usual lately.

At least they are when they pull me over.

I don't want to give you the impression that I'm some kind of maniacal driver who gets pulled over every time he gets behind the wheel. The fact is, I've never even been given a speeding ticket.

Talked myself out of a fair number, but never been given one.

I've also had the opportunity to closely inspect the personal weaponry of several officers. It happened again the other night. I was just trying to make it easier for the officer to hear me, when he reached for his holster.

Try to be nice and look where it gets you.

It was midnight on a Saturday night, when I hit the traffic jam created by a drinking and driving checkpoint near my home. Because the little motor that runs my power window died, I opened the door to speak to the officer.

Wrong move, Bubba.

I guess the officer thought I was opening my door to make it easier to shoot him. He may also have perceived my dog as a bit of a threat. She might have leapt from the car and overpowered him by licking his face, giving me the opportunity to disarm him and make good my devious plot on his life.

He instinctively reached for his gun. I, on the other hand, instinctively knew that I was probably going to have to get my upholstery cleaned.

"Window stuck," I shouted, trying to maintain some degree of composure, articulate speech, and control of my sphincter. "Don't shoot."

The officer kept his hand poised on his holster clip as he bent down to look in the car. "Anything to drink tonight?" he asked, sure that anyone who would try to throw open their door at a drunk driving checkpoint must have put a few back before venturing out on the road.

"No sir," I replied, "but after seeing you go for your gun like that, I think I'll go home and pour myself a very large one."

I did a quick mental inventory of my liquor cabinet and decided that not only was it somewhat deficient, there probably wasn't enough alcohol in the city to settle my nerves.

I'm sure the average gun carried by the average police officer is capable of blowing a hole in the average columnist roughly the size of the Grand Canyon.

On one occasion, several years ago, I got to closely look down the barrel of one of those small automatic weapons that are capable of blowing several dozen holes in the average columnist, in the same amount of time it takes a revolver to blow the single aforementioned hole.

The bank on the ground floor of the office building I was working in at the time, was robbed. Police set up a road block near the building I had to pass through to get home. The police officer inspecting the cars carried one of those small machine guns.

When it was finally my turn to speak with her, she said, "Open your trunk."

I was driving a hatchback at the time and thought I was being helpful by pointing out to her that my car did not have a trunk.

Wrong move once again, Bubba.

She turned, almost imperceptibly, but just enough to leave me staring directly at the open end of the barrel of her machine gun.

"Open the back of your car," she said with a voice that told me she wasn't in the mood for technicalities.

I decided that it might be better to just quietly follow her instructions. I nearly slipped up, but the business end of that automatic weapon made me realize I probably shouldn't ask if her eyes were glazed, because she was pointing a gun at me under the influence of too many donuts.

I'm going to try to avoid similar situations in the future. I've decided that it would probably really ruin my day to have a police officer fire a warning shot or two into my head.

Besides, making that big a mess in the car would really tick off my wife.

Some Turkeys Are Armed

I'm concerned.

While I don't have any trouble admitting I often leave people wondering if my brain is stuck in park with the emergency brake set, I've been running into more people than usual who leave me wondering the same thing.

Let's start with the Minutemen Militia.

Apparently, they feel the need to protect America from Canadians by standing around on the border with guns, and IQ's slightly smaller than the caliber of their bullets.

They claim that the US Border Patrol and the US Customs and Immigration Service agents are not doing an adequate job of protecting America.

From what?

On behalf of all Canadians, I would like to assure America we have no intention of secretly crossing the border and forcing you to switch to the metric system. We will not be demanding service in both French and English at the gas pumps where we fill our cars for twenty percent less than it costs us in Canada. We don't even want to make Americans aware that beer should not have the taste and alcohol content of bottled water.

The part of this that confuses me is that I've met a great many US Border Patrol officers and Customs and Immigrations personnel over the past several years. In virtually every occasion, I've been treated with respect, and still left with the feeling they have been thorough in determining that my dog and I do not represent a threat to the safety and security of the United States.

I do not have any desire to give these people even the slightest inclination I might be a security threat. Let's face it, they're armed and have the authority to look in every conceivable nook and cranny in your vehicle, AND every conceivable nook and cranny in your anatomy.

I don't even like to think about my doctor doing that.

(According to him, he isn't all that thrilled about the idea either; something that gives me a peculiar sense of relief.)

I've often wondered what sort of thing they find when they look into some of those places, and what they would do if they actually found something perfectly legal in there.

"Yes officer, that is a quarter. I keep it there in case I have to use a pay phone or unlock a grocery cart."

Perhaps the Minutemen Militia are on the wrong side of the border. Canada doesn't seem to be nearly so demanding in the kind of people it hires to work along our border with the United States. An experience I had last week would seem to highlight that concept.

I've bought turkeys in the United States for nearly twenty years. They are cheaper, and I think that American turkey farmers must be feeding their birds better tasting chemicals, because we always get a more flavorful bird from the grocery store where we buy them in Lynden, Washington.

When I got to the border, I reported to the Canada Customs officer that I had purchased a turkey. I passed her the receipt from the store to show her I had indeed bought just one bird, thereby abiding by the import rules.

"Well, where's the turkey?" she asked.

Let's see. I was in the driver's seat. My wife was in the passenger seat. My dog was in the back seat. Do you think it just might be possible, if not likely, the turkey would be in the trunk? Perhaps trunks were not something she learned about in customs officer school.

I desperately wanted to say something along the lines of:
- 'I put it under the hood to cook it on the way home. Would you mind taking a look to see if it needs basting?"
- "My wife is sitting on it. She's thawing it out with a hot flash."
- "The poultry one is in the trunk. The human one is in the Canada Customs uniform."

That's when I remembered her gun, and that Canada Customs can look in those same nooks and crannies, and decided that discretion might be the right choice for the moment.

Besides, I couldn't remember if I still had my quarter for the phone call.

Old Friends, Lovers, and Shaky Memories

Being on the road lets me spend some time with old friends as I travel around the country. I've had a few days with two people who have been part of my life for over twenty-five years and it brings back a lot of memories.

I stayed with 'the other woman' in Ottawa last week. Back in the late 1970's, Angela and I worked together in the federal government of Canada. Because we were working on a special project and spending a great deal of time together, my immediate supervisor decided that something must be amiss. He called my wife to tell her I was having an affair.

Luckily for me, Diane knew the truth, but ever since, we've referred to Angela as 'the other woman.'

I called my son from Angela's house the other day and left a message for him to call me at her number. When he did, Angela answered the phone and a somewhat confused son asked who she was.

"I'm the other woman," said Angela.

I think I'll have some explaining to do when I get home.

In Toronto, I got together with my old university buddy, Roy. We go back to our misspent youth in 1973. After all, what good is youth if it can't be misspent?

We decided to take a drive around the campus of our old Alma Mater to try to bring back the memories of our exploits during our days there, so many years ago.

We were amazed at how much the campus had changed. New buildings had sprung up where once were the open fields and forests that witnessed many a late night party. We found our old residence buildings and recalled many of the educational activities we had participated in over our years there.

It probably won't surprise you to know that few of our memories of educational activities actually took place in the classrooms and lecture halls.

Like all great friendships in history, ours had its ups and downs. We tipped bottles up and fell down a lot.

On one occasion, we needed to settle something that neither of us can remember. We were left with no other choice but to fight a duel.

Yes, a real duel, complete with weapons, seconds, and hysterical women. (They were hysterical because they were laughing at us, not because of any great fear that either of us were in any imminent danger.)

At midnight on a hot summer day in 1974, Roy and I stood back to back in the middle of a dusty street, armed with our potentially lethal weaponry.

We took ten steps, turned, and fired. Luckily, we both missed. In fact, based on our state of inebriation, it would have been highly unlikely that either of us could have hit the side of a barn from two paces.

I don't think anyone ever found the ammunition that arced somewhere over our heads and disappeared into the darkness of the summer night. When it was clear we had missed each other, Roy and I had little choice but to put the muzzles of our weapons into our mouths.

It wasn't that we were both feeling suddenly suicidal because of the botched duel. We just didn't want to waste the champagne from the bottles from which we had just fired the corks at one another. It was either put the bottles to our mouths or let it continue spewing forth and onto the pavement at our feet.

Dueling with champagne corks seemed so much safer than any other weapon we might have chosen. Still, I often wonder what would have happened if either of us had been a better shot. I'm not sure how we would have explained it to the emergency room staff, the police, or our medical insurance companies.

Roy and I are thirty years older now and we might even be a little bit wiser. Proof of that comes from the fact we're not predisposed to wasting good alcohol by shooting it at one another in the middle of the street. Our duels today seem to involve: who can consume more alcohol without falling asleep in a lounge chair, who can remember the name of the co-ed who kept her dorm room drapes open all the time, and who can make the other one pass beer through his nose by making him laugh just as he takes a sip.

If you're keeping score, I'm winning. Just don't tell Roy I told you that, because he'd probably say I wasn't being entirely truthful.

He wouldn't be either.

How High's The Water Momma?

If there is a single consistent pattern in my life, it seems to be its inconsistency.

Because I'm spending so much time away from home these days, it would be nice to think my home life might be something that could give me a bit of consistency.

When we sold our house and bought an apartment, we thought the smaller space would give us less work and a place to come home to and relax. There would be no yard to tend, no exterior painting, and no leaking roof to worry about. It would be a carefree existence that would let Diane and I concentrate on our careers. Consistency would be the order of the day.

In a perfect world that might have happened, but we all know the odds of that, don't we?

A few weeks before I started this latest round of touring, our youngest son broke free from the bonds of home and moved into an apartment of his own.

Oh joy. Oh sweet bliss. We had a spare room.

Before we even had a chance to finish thinking about what we might do with the extra space, our oldest son asked if he could move back home for a while.

So much for consistency.

A few weeks later, when I was far away from home, I called Diane. I wanted to know that all was well on the home front, and some degree of consistency existed, making things easier for her, while I was moving from one hotel to another in the inconsistent lifestyle of the touring author.

"Well, we've managed to pull twenty-three gallons of water out of the living room carpet so far," she said, "and it's still pretty wet."

That didn't sound like the consistency I had hoped for.

"When I walked into the living room this morning, I thought the dog had peed on the carpet, but I soon realized she would have needed a bladder the size of Rhode Island to have produced that much liquid," she added.

Apparently, our neighbors had decided to power wash their deck. It's something they do so often, they found it was more economical to go out and buy their own power washer. It's not even that big a deck. Giving it the benefit of the doubt, it might be eight feet by fifteen feet, but that's probably stretching it a bit. Why that takes a power washer is beyond me.

Hearing that power washer every few weeks is one of the consistencies in my home life, though. Apparently, their deck needs to be blasted with pressurized streams of water very frequently.

The odd thing about that pressure washer of theirs is that for some reason it needs to be connected to the tap on my deck. Luckily for them, my tap is located within easy reaching distance of their deck.

When I returned home from the trip, I found my living room in more disarray than I usually leave it. Half the carpet was ripped up. There was a gaping hole in the wallboard. The furniture had all been pushed to one end of the room.

There's nothing like returning to the consistency of home after three and a half weeks on tour, and this was definitely nothing like it.

That was three weeks ago.

The living room still looks the same. We've had to wait until the building association, the building management company, the building's insurance company, the restoration contractor, and quite possibly Santa Claus, the Easter Bunny, and the Lucky Charms™ Leprechaun, decide what to do about it.

I've had to watch the NHL Stanley Cup playoffs on the twelve-inch TV in the bedroom.

That borders on mental cruelty.

I'm told that sometime in the next few days a contractor will be here to redo the carpets, fix the gaping hole in the drywall and repaint the living room.

Sometime.

Even the cable company gives you a better idea of when you might expect to see some action.

Of course, I can probably also expect to hear the neighbor's power washer again, sometime in the next couple of weeks. If and when I do, I will be sorely tempted to go over there and stick its nozzle somewhere the manufacturer doesn't recommend putting it.

That would surely cause some inconsistency.

Or would incontinence be a better word for it?

Sometimes A Drive Down Memory Lane Can Be Scary

It doesn't seem to take much to trigger a vivid memory. It might just be a few notes of a song that sets it off. Driving past a location can bring about a flashback to another time at the same place.

Sometimes they aren't pretty.

My wife and I went for a drive the other day. Living on the coast, we don't see very much snow. From time to time we miss it, and thankfully, we only need to drive a few miles into the mountains to get our fill.

That particular drive is a memory minefield.

On one side of the road dozens of waterfalls cascade down the side of the mountain taking the melting snow down to the ocean. On the other side of the road, the mountain continues its drop to the sea. The road twists and turns, clinging to the edge for almost forty miles.

Remember the part about twisting and turning. It will be important later.

Eventually, the road leaves the coastline to head further into the mountains. Close to that point is a waterfall, taller than Niagara, but only a few feet wide. At its base is a campground. It's that campground that convinced me that it camping is not something that I should do. Every time I drive past it, the memory of my one and only night spent there, floods back into my mind.

Twenty-two years ago, the summer that my oldest son was four, the two of us set off on an overnight camping trip to do some father/son bonding. The campground at the base of the waterfall looked like a good place to spend the night. There were trails to walk along, and just in case my cooking over an open fire was a complete failure, there was a restaurant at the campground gate.

Let me assure you that the base of a huge waterfall is the wrong place to camp with a young child. It wasn't a safety issue. It was a sleep deprivation issue.

Apparently, the lulling sound of water rushing down the side of a mountain has a suggestive effect on the subconscious mind of a four-year-old. Every forty-five minutes throughout the night, Mike woke up with an urgent need to be taken to the restroom, some hundred yards away.

The next morning we broke camp and headed off for a drive further into the mountains, climbing over a mile above sea level, where we had spent the night. Before turning around and heading for home, I bought us each an ice cream cone. Once he laid eyes on it, Mike could not be convinced away from tiger tail ice cream, a combination of bright orange and black. Part way down the mountain he was thirsty. We stopped at a gas station and bought a couple of cans of cola.

Looking back, they may not have been the best purchase decisions I ever made.

As we drove out of the mountains and back along the highway clinging to the edge of the mountain, Mike grew quiet. I assumed he was tired from waking up so many times in the night. I kept my eyes on the twisting turning road.

Remember those twists and turns I said would be important to this story? They were also important to the effect of combining ice cream and cola in the stomach of a four-year-old.

As we rounded one particularly sharp curve, Mike erupted. The cola and ice cream made a sudden, spectacular reappearance, starting at Mike's car seat in the back and covering everything from there to the dashboard.

Unfortunately, the back of my head was part way between his mouth and the dashboard.

It looked like something left over from the prop department on the movie The Exorcist.

I didn't know whether to try to clean up the car or just do the sensible thing and push it off the cliff and into the sea. I reconsidered, when I realized the detrimental effects the second hand cola and tiger tail ice cream might have on marine life.

As Diane and I approached that spot on the highway, I had a sudden flashback to that day so many years ago.

It was all I could do to stop myself from throwing my hands behind my head to protect my neck and hair.

Raindrops Keep Falling On My Dog

It's raining again.

I don't even have to look out my window in the morning to know I will have raindrops falling on my head and running inside the back of my coat when I take the dog for her walk. I'm not psychic. In the Pacific Northwest, it's easy to tell it will be raining again.

It's November.

Our rainy season starts in early January and goes through to late December. This is the rainiest month of the year. We get almost seven inches in November. That's about the equivalent of entire annual rainfall for Arizona, Nevada and Utah.

There are a lot of folk methods of predicting our weather. One of the most popular ones around here says that if you can't see the mountains you know it's raining. If you can see the mountains, it means it is going to rain soon.

I haven't seen the mountains in days.

When it's raining, I'm faced with a rather odd problem. My dog doesn't want to go outside. It doesn't make a lot of sense. She's a Labrador Retriever. They are supposed to like water. Tara didn't inherit that trait from her canine ancestors. She will do just about anything to avoid getting wet.

She makes her feelings quite well known.

If she sees it's raining when I'm taking her out, she will try to dig her claws into the ceramic tile by the door. I'm forced to drag her through.

This is a dog who can communicate a great deal with her eyes. When she is being dragged out into rain, her eyes say it all for her.

"Awe, please, Gord. Don't make me go out there. I can hold it until it stops raining. I don't care if that's not going to be until sometime after Christmas, I can do it. Let's just stay inside where it's dry. I could even try to learn how to use the toilet. Cats are supposed to be able to use a toilet, and we both know I'm smarter than any cat. Come on, Gord. Please. I don't want to get wet..."

Perhaps I *should* try to teach her how to use the toilet. We've already taught her how to bring a roll of toilet paper to the bathroom when the last piece has been used, which is something we've never managed to teach either of our sons.

When she finally does get through the door, she becomes resigned to the fact that she is going to get wet. Like many other females I know, she takes on the attitude that, if she is going to be miserable, than everybody else is going to be miserable.

"Get me wet, and you're going to get wet too."

Her retaliation takes on a number of forms. First, she will take as long as possible to find the perfect place to do what she came out there to do. Just when I think she has found the spot to leave her pee-mail for the other dogs in the neighborhood, she changes her mind and starts looking for a different spot.

Her eyes say, "Gee, Gord, are you getting wet? What a shame. I think I'll take a sniff over by those trees over there. Too bad you don't have a spare hand to carry an umbrella along with your crutches and my leash."

Just when I'm beginning to think there is enough water in my clothes to eliminate the African drought, she decides to bring out her other weapon of retaliation for being dragged out into the rain.

She shakes.

If there was any part of my clothing still dry after the twenty minutes spent looking for the perfect blade of grass for her to pee on, then it will be completely drenched after the shake.

Tara is a large and powerful dog. When she shakes, it looks like a dump truck just hit a large puddle on the highway. People three blocks away wonder why the rain suddenly intensified.

I might get through the rainy season, if I could just figure out how to get the dog to carry an umbrella.

It's Starting

I'm in northern Montana this week, about four thousand feet above sea level. I awoke this morning to a snow-covered landscape.

I don't particularly enjoy snow. Snow, to me, means a great deal of effort to stay vertical when every force of nature is trying to force me to be horizontal. I don't have a great deal of feeling in the bottom of my feet, so I don't necessarily know when they might go out from under me. My crutches can't send me a signal when they might decide to go in completely opposite directions.

My wife, on the other hand, gets quite excited by snow. My wake-up call this morning, included her, standing at our hotel room window singing, "Oh the weather outside is frightful..."

It was a frightful way to wake up, too.

Snow, of course, brings about images of Christmas. I wish I could say it's the first time I've had to think about Christmas this year. The Christmas season has already begun, even though we are still over a week-and-a-half away from Halloween.

Christmas decorations went up in our town in late August this year. They were needed for a movie that was shooting there.

I started seeing an increase of toy ads in prime time in early October. My first Santa-sighting in a TV ad was on October 11th.

I discovered that several aisles of the Costco store where we shop had been turned over to Christmas decorations, lights, wrap, and cards, even earlier. Since Costco's house brand is called Kirkland Signature (I'm sure, as a thank you for all the money we spent there feeding our sons in their teen years), I kept seeing references to "Kirkland Christmas" items throughout the store.

I suppose a great many people use these last few warm weekends for getting ready for Christmas. It's a time that gets used to deal with, what I consider to be one of the most stressful aspects of the season.

Outdoor Christmas lights.

For some, Christmas light stress is caused by a sense of competition with the neighbors. Every neighborhood has someone who has such a collection of candlepower on his house, trees and fence, he can be seen from the International Space Station.

Even more stress comes his way when visions of power bills start dancing in his head.

There are a lot of things I dislike about living in an apartment condominium, but one of the benefits is I don't have to think about outdoor Christmas lights.

Even the thought of hanging like a bat, twenty feet above the rose bushes, in the rain, installing strings of colored lights, used to make me break out in a cold sweat.

When I did have to hang outdoor Christmas lights, it seemed that, no matter how carefully I checked the strings of lights before I mounted them along the eaves, I would always discover that several bulbs remained unlit after the installation was complete.

I'd explain to my sons that I spelled "Joy To The World" or "Merry Christmas" in Morse code. Unfortunately, my wife, the career Girl Guide, can read Morse code. Knowing this, the boys would always turn to her for a translation. It seems, year in and year out, I would always spell, "Your father has a few loose bulbs upstairs."

I once read of a man who took great pains to assure his safety while he hung the lights around the front of his house. He tied a rope around his waist and attached the other end to the trailer hitch on his car, which was parked in the back lane. Unfortunately, his wife didn't notice the rope as she rushed out to get some missing gingerbread ingredients.

No doubt, the sudden tautness of the rope gave him some reason to feel stress. He didn't have much time to think about it. A split second later, he became Lonny the Human Box-kite.

His story was later used in a Christmas movie, but I doubt he got any royalties for his trouble.

So be prepared. The season is already upon us and gaining momentum. Let me be the first to say, "May all your Christmas lights be tight."

The Age Old Christmas Saying: "Pass Me Another..."

My mother, who seemed to have a saying for just about every situation, used to say "Christmas is coming and the goose is getting fat."

I'm not sure about the goose, but there are so many ways to add pounds at this time of year, I know the rest of us are probably fattening up a bit. Shortbread, marzipan, plum pudding, to say nothing of the pounds of chocolate truffles that seem to appear as the holidays get closer, all last a moment on the lips but forever on our hips.

I think I'm still carrying a couple of chocolate hazelnut hedgehogs around that I ate in 1978. I'm even one of the few people you will ever meet, who is actually willing to admit he likes fruitcake – especially if it has been soaked in rum for a good long time, and washed down with more.

Rationalizing seems to be everyone's favorite hobby when faced with a table spread with holiday goodies. We'll enjoy them now, and make New Year's resolutions next week, to take care of the added calories we ingest in the last half of December.

We all know how well that works, don't we?

All of the weight gained over the holidays seems to fly in the face of some of my long-held theories about dietary habits. I don't want to believe it, but it just might be possible that brown foods actually do have calories. It may even be true that calories don't escape from whatever you plan to eating as soon as it's sliced. Accepting those theories has gotten me through a great many situations that might have made me feel guilty about my food intake.

They've also provided me with my rationale for not eating foods that do not fall into those categories. That takes care of a lot of vile and evil foods such as Brussels sprouts and broccoli.

Of course, what would the holidays be if it weren't for a drink or twelve? I've heard scandalous reports that liquor might be laden with calories. That can't be right. How could a drink like Irish whisky have anything but good in it? Even the name comes from the Gaelic, '*uisge-beatha*' which means 'water of life.' Sounds healthy enough, doesn't it? You might even want to put it on your breakfast cereal.

Aside from the water of life, this time of year seems to be synonymous with sharing a few extra beers, a glass of wine or two, and whatever else might suit your fancy. More than a couple of tea-totaling friends of mine have fallen off the wagon at this time of year.

One guy I know insists he is not an alcoholic because alcoholics go to meetings. He avoids all meetings; even the ones at work.

And proud of it.

It all comes to a head on Christmas Day. From the breakfast of cinnamon buns, to the final, all-encompassing display of gluttony around the dinner table, the day is a non-stop festival of indulgence. Candy, cookies, tarts, fruitcake, turkey, trimmings, plum pudding, and more, all disappear with a blink of an eye.

Turkey, as we all know, contains an enzyme called triptophan, which, among other things, makes you sleepy. It always seemed to have a greater effect on guests who used to spend the day with us. When it came time to clean up after the meal, they would find a spot on the couch and fall under the influence of triptophan.

After a few years of this, I suggested they try a different enzyme called triptosomebodyelse'shouseforChristmas.

I was talking to a rather thin doctor friend of mine the other day. I asked him how he managed to stay thin at this time of year. He said that he had a fairly simple, sure-fire way that anyone could follow to avoid the excesses of Christmas.

"I'm Jewish," he said. "You could always think about converting."

I think I'll stick with the problems caused by overeating, rather than even think about circumcision at my age.

So, Christmas is coming and the goose is getting fat, and my wallet is the only thing that is getting thin around here. Whether you are celebrating Christmas, Hanukkah, or Kwanza, I wish you all the best.

Well... I Think It's An Emergency

I've often thought that the whole 911 emergency call system is inadequate. Oh sure, the people who answer the calls do a great job sending the fire department or the paramedics out to assist you, but there are so many more things that they could be doing to serve their communities. Perhaps what we need is a full range of three-digit calling codes to help us get through the other emergencies of day-to-day life.

Naturally, I've a few suggestions.

Dial 211 for missing recipes.

Last Thanksgiving, we were faced with a major culinary crisis. The scrap of paper my mother's pumpkin pie recipe was written on thirty years ago had disappeared. It's a well-known fact that one can't celebrate Thanksgiving without pumpkin pie. It may even be against the law in certain parts of the country. It would have been so much easier if we could have just picked up the telephone, dialed 211, and had someone either tell us where we had last put the recipe or tell us just how much nutmeg my mother used in her recipe. Without that service, we were forced to spend hours tearing apart the kitchen in search of that scrap of paper.

Dial 311 for English-to-teenager translation services.

Now that my sons are in their twenties, we seem to be able to communicate a whole lot easier. It wasn't quite so easy during those turbulent years between 1993 and 2001, when we cohabitated with teenagers. A three-digit emergency calling number would have been invaluable for parents like us who had difficulty understanding the meaning of typical teenage terminology.

I'm sure my wife and I are not the only parents who have had difficulty understanding that, when a teenager says, "OK," it doesn't necessarily mean agreement with whatever you are asking him to do. That simple "OK" could mean anything from, "I'm saying 'OK' just to get you off my back and I'll forget whatever it is you are asking by the time you leave my room," to, "If I say 'OK' to anything you ask now, I'll get to watch that vein pop up on your forehead later when you discover that I didn't really mean I agreed to do it."

Dial 511 for television mediation services.

It was hard enough when the boys lived at home to get control of the television. It seemed that whenever there was something I wanted to watch there was a rerun of the Simpsons that they needed to see, just in case they had missed some of the intellectual nuances the first twelve times they had seen that episode. Now that there's just my wife and I vying for control of the remote, I'm just as likely to end up watching a rerun of Star Trek when I would prefer to watch ESPN. A quick-dial television mediation service might give me a fighting chance to catch a few minutes of a hockey game during the commercials.

Dial 611 for computer explanations.

I don't ask a lot from my computer. I expect it to turn on when I push the button, and I think it's pretty reasonable that it stay on until I'm finished working. I realize that probably sounds pretty naïve to anyone who has even the slightest understanding of how computers work.

When I worked in a large corporate setting, I had staff that always seemed to take a coffee break just at the exact moment when I needed their attention. Apparently, my computer has pretty much the same attitude. Whenever I really need it to do something, it will make the monitor screen turn blue, tell me push CTRL-ALT-DEL, and forget everything I've typed during the previous four hours. When that happens, I should be able to pick up the phone, punch three numbers and be connected to someone who can explain in simple English why. Even if they can't explain why it happens, they could try to talk me out of jumping out my office window when it does.

Dial 711 for retaliation.

I'm sure I'm not alone when I say I would like to be able to punch in three digits on my telephone the next time a telephone solicitor calls me at dinner time. The person at the 711 call center could take the details of my retaliation emergency and respond by calling the telephone solicitor back at 3:00 AM every night for a month.

It's clear that these additional emergency call services are needed because the people at 911 get pretty cranky when I call them with a missing pumpkin pie recipe report.

Eventually We Get To Pay Our Kids Back

There's an amazing thing about having kids. Even though for many years you don't think it will ever happen, they do eventually grow up and turn into adults like the rest of us.

My youngest son is about to turn twenty-three. I'm not sure how that happened. I don't feel that much older than I did when he was born, although one look in the mirror will point out a number of subtle - and not so subtle - changes that have occurred over the past quarter century.

Brad inherited a few things from me and I'm not just talking about his boyish good looks. (OK, he probably didn't get those from me, but a father can pretend.) When people who know me meet Brad they usually make some comment about the nut not falling too far from the tree. Brad shares my sense of humor.

He had a lot of opportunity to develop his humorous bent. Brad was the kid who didn't really need to sleep. Our oldest son started sleeping though the most of the night when he was just a few weeks old. Brad started sleeping through the night when he was a four-year-old.

Many a night he would come into our room, walk to my side of the bed and shout, "Dad! Are you asleep?"

"Do you want to play Lego with me?"

"If I pull your eyelids open will that make you awake?"

If you have any doubts, let me assure you that having a three-year-old pry your eyelids apart will most definitely snap you into a state of being very wide awake.

Half blind, but very wide awake.

I didn't get any sympathy from my wife when he'd do that. I suppose her memories having to get up and feed him in the middle of the night were still too fresh.

I spent the weekend with Brad. The two of us headed off to Seattle where I was speaking at a writer's conference. It had been far too long since we'd had a chance to just hang out together. My work, his university classes, and the arrival on the scene a few years ago of a very lovely girlfriend had reduced those father-son times into a moment here or there when we could make room in our schedules.

When I teach humor writing at writer's conferences I tell people to start out by revealing their most embarrassing moment. I always start out by giving them mine. Having Brad, in the audience for this discussion was a unique experience. He was, after all, the major player in the whole thing.

When he was in three-year-old preschool, he stopped the Christmas pageant dead during the singing of a song and dance routine about putting up a Christmas tree by announcing to the audience and all the ships at sea that he couldn't get his freaking tree into the freaking stand.

Unfortunately for all concerned, especially his father, he didn't use the word 'freaking.' The word he used can't be printed in a mainstream newspaper, but freaking is a fairly close approximation.

I should probably be annoyed that so many people think he was repeating something I had said while putting up our tree. I probably would be if they weren't right.

Still, it was nice to see my audience turn and look at Brad when I related that story on the weekend.

It was also nice to see a slight blush appear on his cheeks.

Sharing a hotel room gave me another chance to get back at Brad. In the middle of the night, I developed a rather painful back spasm, probably due to the long drive in a rental car that I wasn't used to. Brad says he woke up with a start when he heard me make a noise that sounded like the monster in the movie Alien as it exited through the chest of its unsuspecting victims. I can't imagine how he didn't think I was being sincere when I apologized for waking him up.

It may not have been as painful a way to be jolted into wakefulness as having someone pry your eyelids open, but it had the same startling results. It almost made having the back spasms worthwhile.

If The Globe Is Warming, Why Am I Shivering?

My mother used to recite a little poem at this time of year:
Spring has sprung and fall has fell.
Winter's comin' cold as... last year.

I always thought that if she put her mind to it, she could come up with a final word that would make the poem rhyme better.

Her little poem came to mind the other day when I was reading a copy of National Geographic in an airport terminal. Most of the magazine was dedicated to global warming. It foretold of a time in the not too distant future when we might be able to pick up some oceanfront property in Arkansas.

We've been hearing about global warming for the last couple of decades. I'm still not convinced. I was in Calgary, Alberta for an appearance on an early September day and the temperature didn't get above the very low forties all day. I had not come there prepared for temperatures like that.

Where was global warming when I needed it?

In 1991, I was involved in overseeing the filming of a made-for-TV Christmas movie in Vancouver, BC. The filmmakers were trying to disguise Vancouver as Philadelphia, a feat in itself. But trying to make it look like Philadelphia at Christmastime, in Vancouver, in July, was a Herculean task.

Snow was trucked into the downtown core of the city from the mountains. It was used to fill a laneway off one of the busier downtown streets. The snow was then given a top dressing of instant mashed potato flakes to give it an authentic, just-fallen look.

At the same time, Vancouver was hosting a large international environmental conference at the convention center just a couple of blocks away. I was standing on the sidewalk adjoining the snow and instant mashed potato laden laneway, when a delegate from the conference approached the scene. As he got nearer, I could read on his badge that he was from Atlanta, Georgia. I knew he hadn't seen the snow yet, so I decided to watch to see his reaction when he came upon the laneway.

It looked like a scene from a cartoon. His jaw dropped and his eyes opened wide. Clearly, he could not believe what he was seeing.

When he finally glanced at me with a questioning look on his face, I couldn't resist the unspoken straight line he was handing me, and said, "Sure screws up your global warming theory, doesn't it?"

He turned back to the laneway, clearly hoping it was all in his imagination; perhaps caused by a wee bit of undigested gruel, from the conference luncheon. By then the actor, Hume Cronyn, was sitting in a pile of the snow doing a remarkably good impersonation of a frozen-to-death homeless person.

Another smartass remark had formed in my mind, and naturally I wasn't going to waste the opportunity to use it.

"Yep, that hole in the ozone layer is sitting directly overhead today. This sort of thing happens all the time around here."

The conference delegate walked away, clearly shaken by what he saw, muttering to himself something along the lines of, "If I hadn't seen it with my own eyes..."

I realize that whenever I write a column like this, my editors will be getting letters asserting that I'm somehow environmentally retarded. I'm not. In fact I firmly believe that we should all be doing everything we can to reduce or eliminate our impact on the planet. I hope we can return, sooner rather than later, to a time when rivers and streams were clean, and you could look at the stars without having them filtered by the haze coming from the tailpipes of millions of vehicles.

But on a cold day in Calgary in September, with the weather forecaster calling for a possibility of overnight snow flurries, I just can't get that fired-up about global warming.

The article I read said that the weather we will all have in the future used to belong to someone else, somewhere else on the planet. If that's the case, I'd like to put my order in now.

I think I'd like Tahiti's weather, thank you very much.

Thieves Strike Empty Nest - Film At Eleven

I'd like to point out that adults, even the supposedly aged ones like me who have passed our fiftieth birthdays, often show much better memory capabilities than our children. It doesn't matter if the children in question are pre-teens, teenagers, or adult offspring who have managed to make their way back in through the revolving door on an empty nest. I've witnessed less than stellar cognitive abilities through each of those stages.

I've experienced all of those stages of parenthood. Preteens have difficulty remembering that toys are kept in a toy box. Teenagers forget they don't really need a ride to the school that is only three blocks away. Unfortunately, homing offspring don't forget where home is.

The downturn in the economy has had a severe impact on a lot of people. Not the least of these, are the people like my wife and I who have had an adult child return to the nest. Those like us who downsized their nest after it emptied, are now faced with housing their adult offspring in a space not designed for more than two adults and a dog.

We managed to get quite used to the concept of having the place to ourselves after our youngest son moved out for the third time. The apartment didn't seem so cramped, and if we wanted to walk out to the kitchen in our underwear, we could do it without causing irreparable harm to our offsprings' psyches.

(I apologize to those of you who will wake up in the middle of the night tonight screaming because the image of me walking to the kitchen in my underwear invaded your dream state.)

Even though our homing son is well into his twenties, he still hasn't developed a fully functional memory. He can't seem to remember the location or the purpose of the hall closet. My wife and I hang our coats in there. We put our shoes and boots in there, too. You'd think that by doing that we would be providing an example of just what should go behind that door.

No.

Clearly, my wife and I aren't thinking or we don't have our priorities set right. We should know that it takes too much energy to put clothes away. That energy is needed for other more important pursuits. Things like sitting up half the night playing a computer game.

Apparently, he hasn't yet learned that coats and boots don't go in the first location where they can be dropped as soon as possible after entering the home. The fact that the location of choice is in the middle of the route from the living room to my bedroom doesn't seem to bother him. He knows the boots and coat are there, so he won't trip over them.

It's my own fault if I should round the corner from the living room to the hall and trip over his boots. I should have stopped at the intersection, leaned around the corner, and checked to see if there were any impediments to my safe passage that weren't there the last time I walked that route.

If my wife and I get tired of tripping, we put his things in the hall closet where one might think they belong. We are then faced with a panic-stricken wail the next time he needs them.

"Someone has stolen my boots!"

Obviously, a daring band of thieves has made their way into our home and stolen a pair of boots, unpleasantly aromatic ones at that, leaving behind the TV, stereo, and computers, when they made their daring get away.

I'm thinking of using this same thought process myself. Thieves could be blamed for a lot of other disappearances around here.

"Someone stole the leftovers we planned on using for tonight's dinner."

"Someone stole all the ice cubes out of the ice cube tray and left it empty in the freezer."

"Someone stole all the minutes we had on our family-plan wireless telephone program."

"Someone stole forty-seven of the cheese slices from the package of forty-eight I bought three days ago."

"Someone stole the room I planned on turning into my office."

"Someone stole the toilet paper and left the empty roll."

"...again!"

Guilty Until Proven Innocent

Because I live just barely north of the forty-ninth parallel, I find it is useful to keep a mailing address in both Canada and the United States. It normally reduces the length of time by several days for my American mail to get to me.

I received a videotape in my US mail the other day. Since it was in my American Post Office Box, I had to bring it back across the border with me.

That's when the trouble started.

The videotape was fairly innocuous. It was a copy of a TV program I had recorded in Florida last spring. When I got to the border, I dutifully told the border guard that I had received a magazine, several pieces of junk mail, and the aforementioned videotape.

"What's on it?" she asked, using a tone that quickly let me know that her suspicions about me had already been elevated.

I explained the videotapes contents and handed it to her to inspect.

"It don't look like no professional tape," she said, this time letting me know by her grammar that my suspicions about her level of intelligence should also be elevated.

"It's from a TV studio," I said, "They don't package their videotapes like something you would see on the shelf at Blockbuster."

"For all I know you could be bringing in porn, or even child porn," she said, already starting to scribble a note on the pad of forms that meant I would be having an extended visit with the people inside the adjacent offices.

I took the tape inside, and didn't get a whole lot further with my explanation about the contents of the tape in there. I was led down a hall to a room with a video player and a television, so that the customs officer and I could watch the tape together.

All the way down the hall, the sounds of rubber gloves snapping on and petroleum jelly jars opening, ran rampant through my imagination. I knew that customs officers had the right to check out the obscure nooks and crannies in your car, and I was pretty certain that they had a similar right to inspect my more personal nooks and crannies when I got inside the customs office.

Thankfully, the TV production people who sent me the video hadn't decided to play a practical joke on me and send me a triple-X rated video, just to see what my reaction would be.

Over the years, I've become aware of a number of practical jokes played on people attempting to cross a border. They have all had results that have blown into unexpected results, far above and beyond the expectations of the perpetrators.

Many years ago, an acquaintance of mine was being sent to the Middle East, into a country that had only just been on the losing side of a war with Israel. Somewhere between his office and the airport, somebody managed to put a yarmulke (the small headgear worn by faithful men of the Jewish faith) into his suitcase.

No doubt, this act was perpetrated by someone who clearly did not care for the individual, which narrowed it down to a field of roughly thirty million people. The man's stay in the Middle East was cut short after the item was found in his suitcase. It lasted roughly the length of time between landing and the next flight out.

He should be thankful that his neck wasn't also cut short.

The airport security x-rays of another acquaintance's briefcase clearly showed that he was trying to bring a pistol onto an airplane. There was no gun. Someone in his office had pasted a tinfoil cutout of a pistol between two pages in the binder that he was carrying in his briefcase. The prank resulted in a missed flight, a lost contract opportunity, and the complete destruction of the man's briefcase while officers tore it apart in their search for the concealed weapon.

So I guess I got off lucky because there weren't any practical jokers at the production studio that sent me the videotape. Clearly, they are professionals in the way they do their business. For that I'm thankful.

...as are my more personal nooks and crannies.

A Domestic Battle Is A Lot More Fun When You're Winning

Most husbands and wives fight from time to time. Hard as it might be to believe, I'm proud to say that I'm the winner and still champion around here.

Don't get me wrong. I would never presume to say that I've won an argument. It is not possible for husbands to win arguments. Even if they win they lose. As I've said before, if a man speaks in a forest and there is no one there to hear him, he will still be wrong.

When Diane and I fight, there are usually weapons of some sort involved. These include water, rubber bands, and on one particularly memorable occasion, a smallmouth bass.

When we were first married, we lived in a small on-campus apartment in a building for married and graduate students. The operative word in that statement is small. Two people could not walk past each other in the kitchen, and the living room/dining room/ study area was barely large enough for a sofa, a chair and a table. We didn't care. It was our first year of marriage and our first apartment. Small was not going to keep us from having fun.

I don't remember how, but I somehow came into possession of a large box filled with extra-long rubber bands. It wasn't long before temptation took over and I made use of a rubber band, that might now be considered unwise.

In my defense, it was something I had learned from my father.

If someone is deep in thought reading a newspaper, magazine or book, they aren't likely to notice that you have taken aim at their reading material with a rubber band. Hitting said object with the rubber band will not inflict pain, but it will produce a spectacular reaction.

A newspaper, when hit soundly with a rubber band that was pulled to its maximum stretching point before launching it, makes a sound just slightly quieter than a double-barreled shotgun.

Diane usually retaliates, but that is when I'm at my safest. There is roughly a five percent chance that any rubber band that Diane attempts to shoot, will actually hit me or my reading material. In most cases the stretchy weapon, will either fire backwards causing Diane to yelp loudly, or it will hit her thumb as it fires and harmlessly career across the room.

By the time we moved out of that small apartment, the entire box of one thousand rubber bands was empty. Some had made their way through open windows and others had been vacuumed up. In all likelihood, the current tenants of that apartment are still finding thirty-two-year-old rubber bands wedged between shelves or behind rarely moved furniture.

When things get really violent around here, one of us is likely to bring out a WMD – a weapon of mass drenching.

Squirt guns? We don't need no stinkin' squirt guns!

No squirt gun, not even those massive ones that started appearing a few years ago, could ever meet our needs. We have hoses, full tumblers, and that squirty faucet thing on the kitchen sink.

A bit of black electrical tape wrapped around the trigger of that thing can guarantee that the next person to turn on the tap is going to get a surprise shower aimed directly at their midsection.

A few days ago, Diane purchased a bottle of water for our dog when we were out for a drive. I was holding the dog's travel dish while she filled it. Temptation got the better of her, and she "accidentally" slipped, spewing roughly a quarter of the bottle's contents in my direction.

She overlooked the fact that I was holding the dog's water-filled travel dish. Need I say more...

So I retain my position as winner and still champion in the battle skirmishes around here – even if you take that one incident involving a ground-to-ground smallmouth bass missile attack into consideration. I'll admit I lost that battle, but I'm way ahead on points, and the fish got away after sideswiping my glasses and falling back into the water, preventing my immediate retaliation.

Still, every so often, I tell Diane that I'd like to go fishing again.

Mischief Runs In The Family

When people look at my brother and I, they have trouble seeing us as siblings. Jim is about five-foot-nine and I doubt if he would weigh one hundred and fifty pounds if he was soaking wet and holding a ten-pound chicken. I'm six-foot-four, and...well... um...gee...let's see...how should I say this?

When it comes to weight, I'm almost twice the man he is.

Jim is also eleven years older than I am. I suppose that in those eleven years, my mother saved up a lot of building material to come up with someone my size. As it was, she was scarcely over five feet tall herself, and I think that was if she was standing on top of the dog.

Even though there are a lot of differences between us, we also have a lot in common. We both tend to be a bit on the creative side when it comes to finding things to laugh at, especially if a practical joke is involved.

We grew up spending our summers across Gull Lake from the town of Gravenhurst, Ontario, about one hundred miles north of Toronto. It was a beautiful spot. You could only get to our place by boat, so we were often isolated from the rest of the world. We were left to our own devices to entertain ourselves, occasionally with kids from other cottages on the same side of the lake.

Each morning, just as the sun would start to rise over the far end of the lake, a man we did not know would row his boat past our point. We'd see him when we'd get out early to fish for smallmouth bass from the end of the point. He'd never acknowledge us. He was just lost in the effort of his rowing.

Jim came up with a novel way to greet him that the man wouldn't soon forget.

He took a coil of wire from our father's tool shed and ran it down to the end of the point. One end of the wire was attached to a speaker that Jim made in woodshop at school, and the other end to a record player. The speaker was carefully hidden in a juniper bush.

In the Fifties, Jimmy Rodgers wrote and recorded a song called Muleskinner Blues. The opening of the song was a loud call of

"Good morning Captain! Good morning to you! Haw...haw...ha-ha-ha-ha-ha-ha!"

As the rower rounded our point, the needle was put onto the record with the speaker turned up to full blast. Hearing the juniper bush shout good morning and laugh was clearly not something he anticipated.

The man stood straight up in his boat trying to determine what was happening. Obviously he didn't know the safety rule that our parents had drilled into us about the hazards of standing up in a boat.

He promptly fell overboard.

It was several weeks before he was seen rowing on the lake again. When he did, he avoided our point with his undivided attention.

Several years later, Jim had the whole lake buzzing. He learned that with a few simple household items (an aluminum pie pan, a dry-cleaner's bag, and part of one of those barbecue starting flammable cubes) he could make a working hot air balloon.

He set a couple of them off one clear August night. They rose and drifted above the lake. The flames illuminated the air inside the drycleaner's bags, giving them an eerie glow. They bobbed along over the water, drifting in the slight breeze.

In those UFO-mad days of the 1960's, eerie glows floating where they weren't supposed to be could only mean one thing - Gull Lake was being invaded by aliens.

The local police reported several calls about UFO's over the lake that night. Thankfully for us, the barbecue lighting cubes burned out before officers could report seeing anything.

I've to wonder if there aren't still a few old-timers on the lake who have regaled their children and grandchildren with the story about the night they saw the UFO.

One of them might even have heard a juniper bush sing Muleskinner Blues.

Sometimes Our Betting System Actually Works

I've often written about the fact I like horses. I like riding them. I like watching them run in an open meadow. I even like the fact that they will behave like an overgrown puppy if they think there might be an apple in your pocket.

Liking horses and knowing much about them are two different things. I might be able to identify a Clydesdale by its hairy feet, but that's about where my ability in that regard ends. I've no idea how to tell the difference between a thoroughbred and a plow horse.

As a result, I'm not one to go to the track and wager huge amounts on the favorite in the eighth.

A few years ago Diane and I went to Churchill Downs in Louisville, Kentucky, home of the Kentucky Derby. Thousands of race fans poured over the betting odds of every race. I poured several glasses of Kentucky's finest bourbon down my throat instead.

I'm not all that certain, but I think I probably came out further ahead than most of my companions, but the bourbon clouded that memory.

Whenever I've placed a wager on a horse, it has managed to make its way around the track, politely letting the other horses lead the way. Several horses I've gambled on have barely beaten the ambulance that followed the racers around the track.

Diane has her own betting system. She watches the horses parade out toward the starting gate, and then bets on the prettiest one.

It had been quite a while since we'd gone to a track, when we decided to go last week for a change of pace. I was prepared to sit through the races with a drink in my hand, and my wallet firmly closed, unless I saw a horse I really was convinced would win.

The event did not get off to the best start. We had not checked the racing schedule before heading out, and got to the track just as the second last race was being called to the post.

We took a seat and ordered what would be our only round of drinks for the day. So much for trying to repeat my beer, bourbon, and scotch trifecta.

We watched the parade of horses preparing for the final race. I could here all of the people around us talking about a mare named Zinzee, and it was clear that the majority of them had picked her to win. As the horses passed our seats, one caught my attention. While the other horses were being well behaved, walking calmly toward the starting gate, a brown filly named Flying Chockli danced down the track. It also lightened its load by dropping a couple of pounds of second-hand hay and oats on the track.

Surely that would give it an edge over the more discrete horses with better bowel control.

Just ahead of the horse I was watching was a gray horse named Diamond Finish. Diane decided that she was going to bet on it to place, because it was the prettiest one in the race. Since she was going to go up to the betting window anyway, meaning that I would not have to leave my drink, I gave her a bill and asked her to put it on the dancing mare for me.

It was clear that our seat mates were not impressed with our bets. For that matter, neither was anyone else in the stands. When the race began, my horse was at the bottom of the odds, just behind the one Diane picked.

Zinzee was impressive from the start, leading through the first thee quarters of the race. Just as I said something about our poor luck picking horses, there was some movement out on the track. Flying Chockli and Diamond Finish started to pass the other horses.

They crossed the line one and two. Dancing ability, a good bowel movement, and looking good won out over the so-called smart money.

I just wish that bill I gave Diane was bigger than a five, but at least it covered the bar bill.

Barely.

My No-Nonsense Wife And Her Non-Sense Of Direction

My wife has a great deal of sense.

Many husbands, especially those who, like me, make their livelihoods in comedy, wouldn't admit that. I've absolutely no problem extolling my wife's good sense.

It sort of balances off our relationship. She has sense and I've nonsense.

We are a little like the fly and a bee trapped on a window. I'm the fly. She is the bee. When a fly is in that situation, it will fly all over the place trying to find a way out. A bee, on the other hand, will take meticulous care and fly straight at the window in an orderly pattern of straight lines. Flies are more creative in their approach. Bees tend to get headaches a lot.

Diane says she often feels like banging her head against something because of me.

She has great common sense. She can look at a decision and seem to immediately know the right course of action that should be taken. Even if I don't necessarily agree with her, I know she is likely to be absolutely right because, let's face it, I'm most likely to be wrong.

Better still, she has great financial sense. That's a good thing, and not just because I'm easily swayed by things that involve spending money. Diane tempers that character flaw on my part. She doesn't even let me carry checks because I firmly believe that as long as I've checks that haven't been written on, there must be money in the bank account.

Apparently, it doesn't always work that way.

Who knew?

Another reason her financial sense is an asset is because she has turned it into a very successful career as a stock broker.

I may have three books out, a syndicated column and a comedy CD, but so many people around home are her clients that I get referred to as Mr. Diane Kirkland.

She even has a pretty good sense of hearing. She can hear things that the average human can't. As a result, if anyone in the neighborhood blows one of those "silent" dog whistles, her hair will stand straight on end. She can also hear the silent alarms in jewelry stores, so that, combined with the aforementioned financial sense, keeps her from doing too much bling-bling shopping.

Of course, nobody is perfect. She does have one major flaw in her sense inventory.

Diane has the sense of direction of a drunken raccoon with its head stuck in a honey can.

We were recently in a casino in Las Vegas. Diane walked in a straight line from where we were sitting to the restroom about seventy-five feet away. I found her twenty minutes later at the far end of the casino, still trying to figure out where we had been sitting with all those slot machines that "all look the same" beeping and clanging all around her.

After the third time this happened, I threatened to get a helium balloon and tie it to her wrist so she'd be easier to find.

We've lived in the same area for twenty-three years. When the call display feature on my office phone shows she is calling me from her car, I don't even bother to say hello anymore.

"Where are you going, and how lost are you?" are the first words I say.

I've to admit, from time to time I will lose my way from point A to point B. I won't say I get lost, I simply get directionally misaligned. I firmly believe that as long as I know which state or province I'm in, I can't possibly be lost. I've always managed to find my way to wherever I'm going. It just might take a bit longer and follow a more circuitous route to get there.

I don't need to swallow my pride or damage my sense of masculinity by stopping and asking for directions.

That's because I've a sense of direction.

Diane, on the other hand, has the sense to ask directions. Just don't ask her to give them or be your navigator.

There's just no sense.

Driving Miss Adventures

I usually find driving to be a fairly relaxing activity. It would be even more so if other people would just stay off the roads.

For me, getting into the car and going for a drive has always been a way of life. As a child, long hours on Fridays and Sundays were spent driving to and from the family summer cottage. Early in our marriage, the commute to work was approximately forty miles each way from the small hobby farm we bought. Today, I find one of the best cures for the writer's block that can affect all of us in this business, is to get in the car and go for a drive.

This love for driving means that on any given Sunday, Diane and I will get in the car and head out onto the road, as the old Chuck Berry song used to say, "with no particular place to go."

A couple of recent events might make a normal person wonder about the sensibility of that particular pastime, but I've never been accused of being anything resembling normal or sensible.

Last weekend, on a drive to a store in Bellingham, Washington, my car's alternator decided to stop alternating, or whatever it is that an alternator is supposed to do. The odd thing was that it had the exact same problem on the exact same road four years ago. Something along that road is opposed to my alternator's lifestyle.

Another recent driving misadventure occurred when Diane and I were in Las Vegas a couple of weeks ago. We decided to take a break from the neon lights, street-corner timeshare salespeople, and the constant din of slot machines by renting a convertible and heading out into the desert.

We left Vegas at seven o'clock in the morning, and returned the car at midnight after adding over seven hundred miles onto its odometer.

It was a gorgeous day to be out in a car with the roof down. The temperature was warm and the sun shone down on us, as we headed east from Las Vegas, past the Hoover Dam and on into the Arizona desert. Heavy rain the previous week had made wildflowers blossom, turning parts of the desert into seas of purple and yellow.

By late afternoon, we reached Sedona, Arizona. We waited there to watch the sun set on the outcroppings of red rocks, cliffs, and cacti. It was still quite mild as we headed north towards Flagstaff and the interstate that would take us back to Las Vegas. I left my jacket in the back and we kept the roof down on the car.

I suppose it would have been smart to look at the map before heading out of Sedona at dusk. We might have seen that the road took a winding route north rising to some seven thousand feet above sea level, before dropping down into a narrow canyon. Apparently, at this time of year, the sun doesn't reach the bottom of the canyon during the day, keeping the temperature much cooler than the surrounding area.

As we drove, we kept a constant eye on the flashing light on the dashboard that indicated the rapidly dropping outside temperature. When we left Sedona, it was in the mid-sixties. By the time we had driven less than fifteen miles along the road to Flagstaff it had dropped to the upper-thirties.

To make matters worse, another driver chose to drive along the route at twenty miles per hour. That gave us plenty of opportunity to experience the onset of hypothermia in the open convertible. Because the road twisted and turned along the canyon floor, we were unable to pass the dawdling driver ahead of us. We also had nowhere to pull off, put up the roof, or get my jacket.

On most of our drives we see or learn something new. I've learned that I should probably stay away from the road in Washington that seems to have a negative affect on my alternators. On the road north of Sedona I learned something else.

Shivering can be a form of aerobic exercise.

Snow Isn't Fit For Man Nor Beast

In 1996, I wrote a column about the problems we face in the Pacific Northwest when we have to deal with snow. In the twenty three years I've lived on the coast, I've only had to deal with a few snowstorms. As a result, snow scares the bejeezus out of me as much as it does the people who have spent their entire lives out here.

That particular column was called *Disaster Strikes Vancouver - Many Left Without Access To Cappuccino*. For many of the residents of this area, a disruption in the supply of caffeinated beverages is one of the worst things that could happen to them.

We've just come through one of those periods of snowy weather. For much of the last ten days, most of the region has been all but shut down by a horrific dump of snow.

We got nearly four inches.

The Greater Vancouver area is home to approximately two million residents. There are about twenty snowplows to serve the entire area. I think that one or two people might actually own a snow shovel, but they are just people who moved here and forgot to leave it behind when they packed up their belongings.

I've a special reason for disliking the snow. When it arrives, I am, for all intents and purposes, placed under house arrest. My crutches seem to develop a mind of their own on icy sidewalks. My wheelchair is just as useless, although it might be better if I could find a little set of chains to go on the tires.

I spoke to a police officer in Seattle during a snowstorm a few years ago. He said that there are three kinds of drivers in the snow. There are the people with old or economy cars who drive with extra caution because they don't want to run into a luxury car or a truck. There are the people with luxury vehicles who drive with extra caution because they don't want to be hit by someone in an economy car. Then there are the people with SUVs who think that their vehicle can do anything in the snow, rain, mud or sleet.

"Take a look as you go along the highway," he said. "Eight out of ten of the vehicles parked upside-down in the median will be SUVs."

It's not just the human population that suffers when snow comes to the Pacific Northwest. Animals seem less able to deal with it than their relatives in other parts of the county.

Tara, my assistance dog, is supposed to keep me standing up on my crutches. When she sees snow on the sidewalk she gives me a look that clearly means, "All bets are off, Gord."

Because of the snow, I had to drive her to her favorite spot to take care of business one day last week. For some reason, this dog, likes to poop on a hill, and seemingly the steeper the better. Like many other dogs, she has a habit of kicking with her back legs after she has completed the job at hand (or in this case I guess it would be better to say 'at paw.')

She learned a valuable lesson that day: it is not wise to kick your back legs out behind you, when you are standing on snowy hill, in a squatting position. As soon as her back legs were off the ground, her front legs lost their footing and she careened downwards without even a modicum of control.

If dogs could blush, she would have been crimson.

Tara is a dog with a long memory. She was stung by a wasp two years ago and still won't walk past the window at the post office where it happened. I'm a bit concerned about what this latest calamity that has befallen her will do to her psyche.

Just this morning, when I asked her if she wanted to go for a walk, she gave me a pensive look that seemed to say, "Y'know, Gord, I bet if you got me a magazine I could learn to sit on the toilet the way you do."

Yeah, sure. Like she could hold a magazine.

I'm Allergic To My Allergies

I'm allergic to June and usually to a good part of July, as well.

Forget trying to decipher the individual allergens that affect me during those weeks. I'm just allergic to the whole period. Grass, flowers, trees, birds and small furry animals all join forces during these early weeks of summer with one purpose in mind:

Making my life miserable.

My eyes burn. My nose runs. My ears feel plugged, and even my gums ache. That's to say nothing of the headache and lack of sleep.

Actually, the lack of sleep is only an indirect symptom of my allergies. Apparently, when my allergies get bad, I have a tendency to snore. I can't personally vouch for this, but every few minutes my wife wakes me up to tell me to stop snoring. Either it's in her imagination, which isn't altogether outside the realm of possibility, or my allergies are making me snore.

Either way, having Diane wake me up so often is murder on my sleep pattern.

I'm afraid to look in a mirror. My eyes are so red I look like something out of a Stephen King movie.

I've tried all manner of hay fever antidotes. I've been buying so much antihistamine this year that the authorities are beginning to suspect that I might be running a crystal-meth lab. In fact, I've tried so many that I may not be allowed to operate heavy machinery until sometime in the year 2012, although since I've never had a call to operate heavy machinery in the past, that shouldn't be too much of a problem.

I think several of the antihistamines I've been taking also preclude me from participating in the Olympics. Again, it isn't likely, but if they were to add a medal category for competitive television watching, I'd hate to be disqualified because of traces of banned substances in my pee.

My dog isn't being particularly helpful with this problem. Any other dog will go for its walk, pick a spot, and do that which it goes for a walk for, without much hesitation or thought about the whole process.

Not Tara.

To begin with, Tara is a Labrador. I've written before about how I'm convinced that crop circles are caused by Labradors trying to find a place to pee. She will circle ten or more times to get just the right spot for posting her pee-mail for the other dogs in the neighborhood, and that's after checking out and disqualifying several other locations first.

Tara also has privacy issues. Any other dog wouldn't give a moment's hesitation before doing her canine duty. Tara does not want to be seen. She has to find tall grass or some bushes to hide behind. That means dragging me through tall grass or into bushes, because I'm on the other end of the leash.

And what do we find in tall grass or in bushes? (OK, well that too, but I can usually get it scrapped off the bottom of my boots before I get home.) The real problem is that, aside from the deposits that other dogs may have left behind, the tall grass and bushes are filled with pollen, and much of it gets sent airborne by Tara when she is creating her crop circles, or, as the case may be, crap circles.

All of that pollen heads directly for my eyes and sinuses. This morning I sneezed twenty-seven times between the far end of our walk and home. I've got to teach that dog how to use the toilet before I give myself whiplash.

Apparently, I'm not alone. A recent report indicated global activities have given rise to a worldwide increase in allergy suffering. Bombs, military vehicles driving through deserts, and other such activities, have all created a significant increase in the quantity of allergens floating around in the air. Even though it's going on half a world away, these minute particles are floating on the breeze and, like some kind of microscopic smart bombs, are all targeting my nasal passages. So, if for no other reason than the sake of my sinuses, please, let's end this war now.

And, could I get a volunteer to walk my dog?

It's Not Like I'm Spoiling My Dog

I want to make it clear that I'm not one of those people who put ribbons in my dog's hair, or paint her toe nails. Still, there are those who say I dote on Tara, my Labrador, a little bit more than is necessary.

Others say she is downright spoiled.

I beg to differ.

She's just provided with an excess of things that she might not really need, but certainly does enjoy.

Tara works hard for her treats and toys. She is trained as a service dog to help me walk by giving me additional stability on my left side, the one that has been affected the most by my spinal injury.

If I drop anything she picks it up for me. I like to think that it is good training that has taught her to do those things, but there may be some validity to the idea that she would rather pick up the car keys than try to get me back on my feet after doing a pratfall when I try to pick them up myself.

I do fall over a fair bit. In fact I'm quite proficient at it. I haven't missed the ground once.

When that happens, Tara is there to help me get back up.

On a similar vein, if I need something on the bottom shelf of a store, Tara will grab it and pass it to me.

Tara has an even more important job, one that anyone who works with a dog sleeping at their feet can attest to. Every so often she will tell me it's time to stop working and smell the dog biscuits, or go for a walk so she can get the pee-mail left behind for her by her local canine buddies.

In return for all her hard work, Tara gets treated very well - some would say, spoiled.

Early in her life, Tara showed a strong affection for stuffed animals. Some dogs just chew them, others-like the late-great dumbest dog to ever get lost on a single flight of stairs who shared my life for thirteen years before Tara arrived - use them as sexual surrogates.

Tara takes very good care of her stuffed animals. Some of them are now three or four years old, and are still in pretty good shape, despite being carried through the house on a daily basis, or used as pillows for her naps.

OK, maybe she has more than she needs. Who's to say? Is one too few, or is eighteen too many?

In my defense, eight of them came out of one of those machines you see that has a hook you try to use to grab a stuffed animal. It was in my hotel a few weeks ago. I saw that one of the toys looked like it might be easy to grab, so I thought I would try to get it for her. When the hook grabbed the bear it caused a landslide inside the machine, and I hit a jackpot of stuffed animals.

For some reason that never happens when I use a slot machine.

Every trip to the pet store means I've to get her another box of canine breath fresheners. We discovered them at a dog trade show a couple of years ago, and she will do just about anything to get me to open that box.

Buying breath fresheners isn't spoiling her. It's self-defense.

I may have gone a bit over the top for her the other day. Even so, I can still rationalize this latest purchase as doing something that will provide her with enjoyment and a healthy source of drinking water.

Sitting on our kitchen floor, after nearly an hour of trying to decipher the instruction manual, is a new dog water dish that constantly circulates the water through a charcoal filter and cascades it back into the dish to keep it oxygenated.

I contend that buying her this high-tech water dish isn't spoiling her. It's not like it refrigerates the water as it flows through the system.

I still have to add ice cubes every couple of hours to do that.

The Abuse Still Cuts Close

I saw a child the other day who was clearly the victim of one of the most insidious forms of child abuse. It's a form of abuse that is prevalent throughout North America and, to make matters worse, child welfare agencies do not consider it to be worth their time or effort to try to prevent it from occurring.

Seeing the boy brought back terrible memories from my childhood that included tears and a lot of begging on my part and a lot of yelling on my father's part.

No child should ever be victimized by a home barber kit.

I'm not sure why or how some people take the giant leap between buying a pair of scissors and an electric clipper and assuming that they can do what barbers and hair dressers go to school to learn. One thing is certain the amount of knowledge that the three page pamphlet inside the package delivers should make even the most cost conscious parent decide that that cutting hair is better left to the professionals.

It's easy to spot the children who are being victimized by this form of child abuse. Some of them have tufts of hair sticking out in odd places; others have every single follicle cut to the exact same length.

I fell into the latter category. My father felt that if he turned on the clippers and ran them over my head several times, I would have good haircut. As a result, thanks to a cowlick that no amount of hair oil could control, I ended up with a head that was roughly the same shape as the nib of a felt tip pen.

Let's just say it was not a good look for me.

If you saw a child today with hair like mine was you would probably immediately assume that he was getting chemotherapy treatments.

I blame John Lennon and my sister for the presence of a home barber kit in my life.

In 1964 The Beatles hit the stage of the Ed Sullivan Show. My sister thought that her brother should follow their lead and have what people were referring to as a Beatle cut. She accompanied me on my next trip to the barbers and convinced him to leave my hair longer at the sides so that it would grow in and look just like Lennon's.

I was ten and she was sixteen, so it was clear to me that, due to her elevated status as a high school student, she must have known what she was talking about. I thought the idea of having hair like someone on TV sounded pretty neat. Had I known then what I knew a few days later, I would have protested that no length of hair was going to worth the pain that was to follow.

The arrival of the home haircutting kit was one of the darkest moments of my childhood. It scarred me for life, and I'm not just talking about the occasion when my father slipped with the scissors a little too close to my earlobe.

Perhaps those years that I spent with hair that had to grow in for a few days before it could be measured is why I relished in the opportunities to let my hair grow longer in my teens and adulthood.

My father was never too pleased with my long hair but by the time I was in my mid-teens I was eight inches taller than him and he chose his battles more carefully. He still occasionally made comments about my hair length or the clothes that I was wearing.

It was quite disconcerting to hear my father's words coming from my sons' lips when I decided to let my hair grow in again a number of years ago.

"You're not going out looking like that are you?"

"Don't you think it's about time you had a hair cut?"

I still get my hair cut every four weeks. Whenever Gary, my stylist, fires up the clippers, I have a flashback to those horrible days in my kitchen facing my father armed with his clippers and his How To Cut Boys' Hair instruction pamphlet.

Abuse like that should be clipped – or at least given a trim around the split ends.

I Don't Ho

Elmer "Len" Dresslar Jr. passed away a couple of weeks ago. That name may not jump out as one that is as recognizable as some, but you've probably heard him laugh thousands of times over the years.

Dresslar gave The Jolly Green Giant his "Ho Ho Ho."

That laugh has followed me for years. Anyone who is significantly taller than average will know what I mean. When you are tall, people take one look at you and say "Ho Ho Ho. It's The Jolly Green Giant."

I think some of them actually think that they are the first ones to ever think of it.

For the record, I am not now, nor have I ever been green. (OK, there was that one time in a small plane in heavy turbulence, but that's another story.)

According to statistics, the average North American male is somewhere between five-foot-ten and five-foot-eleven.

I'm six-foot-four, so you see the problem.

Complete strangers seem to have no qualms asking any number of questions that I have heard hundreds of times before, such as, "How's the air up there?" My stock answer is that the air at my level is probably somewhat clearer because it is further removed from the air pollution caused by flatulence that must be problematic at lower levels.

At social events, when the question of my height comes up, I usually tell people that I am five-foot-sixteen. It gives me a chance to escape to another part of the room while they stop to mentally do the math.

I was six feet tall by the time I was twelve and stopped growing sometime around the age of sixteen. During those years, one of the inevitable questions that I would be asked was, "So how did you get to be so tall?" That question came up so frequently because the rest of the family did not share the height gene. My father was five-foot-eight and my mother claimed to be five-foot-two, but in reality, she would have needed a pair of elevator shoes to be anywhere near to being truthful about that.

Frankly, I have no more idea how I came to be so tall than short people have about how they came to stop growing, although through the years there have been several references to a very tall milkman delivering to our house in the early Fifties.

I've never really understood why shorter people seem so consumed by a need to ask questions about a taller person's height. Tall people don't go around asking "How's the air down there?" or "So why didn't you ever grow past the height of the average fifth grader?"

Oh sure, there are advantages to being tall. I can reach things on the shelves in the kitchen cupboards that my wife would need an extension ladder mounted on a chair to access, but there are a lot of disadvantages, too. The world really is made for people of average height.

Try buying pants when you have a thirty-five-inch inseam.

If I walk into most of the chain clothing stores, the salespeople just look at me and say, "Uhhhh... No," before I even have a chance to say what I'm looking for.

Being tall can be a physically painful experience; something that shorter people never have to contend with.

I parked a car in an underground parking lot beneath the sign for the rental car agency I was returning it to a couple of weeks ago. When I got out of the car the top of my head and the bottom of the sign met rather spectacularly before I had even had a chance to fully stand up. Thankfully, I have a complete collection of words that I save for just those kinds of situations, none of which can be reprinted in a mainstream daily newspaper, and I used every single one of them.

Some of them two or three times.

While I mentally tried to count my fingers, remember what year it was, and all the other tests to see if I had sustained a concussion, I can assure you that I did not feel the least bit like quoting Elmer "Len" Dresslar Jr.

I wasn't in the mood to Ho.

Let Sleeping Dogs Lie In A Public Restroom

I often quote the late Lewis Grizzard when I'm talking to groups of people who would like to write humor. I was a great fan of Grizzard's work, and was saddened to see him go at such a young age.

He said, "When you want to write humor, you really only have to look from the front of your eyelids forward, and pretty soon you are going to see something funny happening that you can write about."

That statement has been proven to be true time and again, leading me to write about the humor in the sights and sounds of everyday life, every week for over eleven years.

And it just keeps happening.

Tara, my assistance dog, and I, recently entered a public washroom. I usually try to avoid them when Tara is with me, because she really lets me know that it is not her favorite place to go. There have been times when I've had to physically drag her through the door. On this occasion, getting in wasn't the problem. It's what went on inside that is going to last in my memory for a long time to come; probably in Tara's, too.

She usually reclines on the floor and uses the opportunity to catch up on her sleep. When she is working at keeping me upright, she has to be fully alert, so she uses every opportunity she can find to grab forty winks.

After a few minutes, a man entered the next stall. It's unlikely that he will forget the events of the next few moments anytime soon, either.

As he sat down, he made a certain noise that you can all use your imaginations to identify. He wasn't quiet about it. In fact, I've heard the trumpet-calls used to announce the beginning of a horse race that don't produce anywhere near the same tonal quality or volume.

Tara rose from her reclining position like a helicopter lifting off. The hair all the way along her spine stood straight on end and she started barking.

I don't think the man was aware that there was a service dog in the next stall. He screamed, and that set off even more barking on Tara's part.

It was unusual, because Tara rarely barks. She might woof if someone is walking past my window, assuming she is awake enough to tell there is someone there. She will also occasionally bark if I haven't thrown her ball quickly enough during play-time.

This wasn't just a woof, or a bow-wow. She started doing an impersonation of the pit-bull that lives down the street from us. It's the kind of bark that indicates someone in the immediate vicinity might be in danger of having their throat ripped out. She made it clear who her intended victim would be, if I would just let go of her harness.

It was obvious she had something to say to this person. It also wasn't too hard to translate just what she was saying.

"Hey! Hey! Hey! Hey! Hey! Hey! Some of us actually rest in a restroom!"

"Hey! Hey! Hey! Hey! Hey! Hey! I have a very sensitive nose!"

"Hey! Hey! Hey! Hey! Hey! Hey! If you're going to do that, at least have the decency to go outside and hide in the long grass like I do."

"Hey! Hey! Hey! Hey! Hey! Hey! You need to switch to a better brand of kibble."

I tried to stifle Tara's barking, but aside from whatever else, Tara had obviously caught the scent of fear and was using responding to it with even more barking. Nothing I could say would stop her.

Of course, it didn't help that I was also having difficulty stifling my own laughter. It's hard to chastise your dog, when tears are streaming down your face, and you are just about having convulsions trying to prevent your laughter from being audible.

It will be a while before I can get Tara through a restroom door again. She tends to have a long memory about things that startle her. I'll bet you can say the same about the guy in that next stall, too.

The Curse Of The Gadget-Addicted

I come from a family that suffers from a serious gadget addiction. Whenever we see something new or unusual, we enter a trancelike state, and begin muttering a mantra of "Must have... oooh shiny... must buy one now... what does it do?... who cares?"

As a result, my brother, sister and I've an odd assortment of things that can best be described as useless, but cool.

My brother suffers the most from this addiction. If he had a coat of arms, I'm sure it would bear the Latin slogan, "Vene, Vidi, Visa."

"I came, I saw, I did a little shopping."

Jim is the only person I know who has purchased a square egg maker. That little device applies pressure to a hot, hard-boiled egg, turning it into a cube. When cooled, the egg could be sliced into squares that fit neatly on a saltine cracker.

I'm still trying to identify the purpose of the gift he gave me for Christmas last year. It looks like something Martha Stewart might have carved from an old toothbrush while she was incarcerated.

My sister is better, but just marginally. Over the years, I've received gifts from Lois that include a fishhook straightener and a set of tongs to hold lit matches so that you don't burn your fingers when lighting birthday candles.

It should come as no surprise then that we all have electric fly swatters. (Mine was a gift from Lois.) Why use an ordinary swatter when you can zap flies, mosquitoes, and spiders into oblivion with the same kind of power that Florida used on Ted Bundy.

When an insect comes into contact with the swatter it either explodes with a loud bang, or it bursts into flame. Even though I know it will bring down the wrath of the folks at the People for the Ethical Treatment of Animals upon me (again) I have to say that it does give a certain feeling of satisfaction to electrocute a mosquito before it can invade your capillaries.

Obviously, with that much power, one has to be very careful with such a device. It has the usual label on it advising it be kept out of reach of children, but mere warning is just not sufficient.

For example, my brother learned the hard way that you should not carry the swatter with the business end under your arm unless you are very sure that it is turned off. We're still not entirely convinced he will ever have underarm hair on that side again.

There should also be a label, clearly indicating it is unwise to let your wife anywhere near you if she is holding an electric fly swatter. It may not be a problem in your household, but I'm married to a woman who likes to see how well things work. It's unhealthy to let her curiosity get the better of her when she's holding an electric fly swatter.

Perhaps the label should just have Diane's picture on it and the words, "Keep out of reach of this person, or failing that, keep yourself out of her reach."

Because of the spinal injury, I do not have a whole lot of feeling on the bottom of my feet. Diane decided to see what would happen if she touched my foot with the swatter.

While I did not feel the spot where she touched me with the swatter, I certainly felt the electricity pass through the rest of my body. I think it might have exited through the bridge of my nose. My heart may have been unnecessarily defibrillated.

I thought other things were going to exit from my body at the same time. My hay fever momentarily cleared up, but that's probably because the sinus congestion was vaporized.

My brain went into overdrive, madly digging up every example of foul language that had ever been stored there to be used at just such an opportunity.

Unfortunately, my mouth did not cooperate and it all came out sounding something like,"Gaaaaaazzzznghunmofffbbbbtpufld orgh."

Diane says she's sorry for trying to electrocute me. I'd find that a lot easier to believe if she could just stop giggling when she says it.

Emergency Preparedness: Hold The Phone Away From Your Ear

My assistance dog can open doors, push elevator buttons, and several other useful tricks, but I've never thought to teach her how to use the telephone.

I'd be afraid she might start ordering pizza.

I recently read a news report about a woman in New Jersey who had trained her German shepherd to dial 911. Apparently, sometime in the middle of the night, the dog made three calls to 911. All they could hear was panting on the other end of the line. They sent three squad cars and an ambulance rushing to the woman's home.

She was arrested for public mischief when they discovered there was no emergency, and that, all along, it was her dog who was making the crank calls.

I can just picture the dog looking at the officers thinking, "No emergency? Did anyone bother to check my supper dish?"

I've had my own problems with 911 lately.

I was driving a freeway near my home the other day. As I rounded a curve I was faced with a large piece of metal ductwork in the middle of my lane. I managed to miss it, but, being the concerned citizen that I am, I decided to call the police to get rid of the hazard.

Perhaps my first mistake was using my wireless phone while I was driving. I called 911 and got an answering tape. It was not what I expected.

"Thank you for calling the 911 emergency service. The following is for the deaf community..."

What happened next was quite unexpected and nearly caused me to put my car into the median. It also made me think that it was about to make me join the deaf community.

A tone erupted from my earpiece that sounded similar to the sound you hear when you accidentally dial a fax number instead of a telephone number. It squawked and squealed directly into my ear canal. Perhaps it wouldn't have been so bad if I didn't have the volume turned all the way up.

Before I could get the earpiece ripped off, a voice came through saying, "911. What is the nature of your emergency?"

I nearly forgot.

Then I wasn't sure if I should tell her about the ductwork on the freeway or the blood that must have surely been flowing out of my eardrum.

"There's a duct on the freeway westbound near the number 52 interchange," I said.

"There's a duck on the freeway?" she asked.

"No. Not a duck. A duct. I saw a big duct sitting in the middle of the carpool lane," I corrected.

"You don't have to shout, sir," she said.

I didn't realize I was shouting, but that is probably because I had just been deafened by the special tone for the deaf community. I was beginning to think she had also been listening to that special tone a little too often, as well.

I was convinced of the fact when she asked, "Is it more like a goose?"

Eventually I got passed on to someone who could grasp the concept of a duct on the road without picturing something with feathers.

I've to wonder if the reason the 911 operators in New Jersey heard so much panting when the German shepherd was calling, was due to that tone. As we all know, dog's ears are much more sensitive than ours. That way, they can tell that Timmy has fallen down a well from a long distance.

I'm all in favor of the 911 system making itself accessible to the deaf community. That tone is required to make the connection to their special telephones. Better that, than shouting, "Hey deaf person. What's your emergency?"

I just think they should make the message a bit clearer.

Something like, "We're about to transmit a mind numbing tone over the phone just in case you might be a deaf caller. If you are not deaf, hold the phone as far away from your ear as possible. If you are on a wireless phone with an earpiece inserted into your ear canal, turn the volume down for ten seconds.

...and If you are a German Shepherd, run to another room."

Heat Kills

I'm in heat.

I've been in heat for the past several weeks.

Before you get the wrong idea, I'm talking about climate conditions. Global warming has been following me around like a lost puppy.

I did an appearance in Cincinnati three weeks ago. The temperature and humidity combined to create a humidex of one hundred and eighteen degrees Fahrenheit. Let's face it; we're talking about a temperature that is over halfway to the boiling point. We are not supposed to live like that.

That morning I was a guest on a TV show. In the afternoon I was on a radio program. In the evening I did a reading and signing at a bookstore. My rental car's air conditioning was just barely making the drive to these places bearable. Getting out of the car was the problem. I was convinced that somewhere between the car door and the TV studio door I would be turned into a puddle on the asphalt.

OK. It would have been a pretty big puddle, but I still contend that it wouldn't have been big enough to call it a pond.

Everywhere I went, people were saying, "It's not the heat. It's the humidity."

They were wrong.

Wrong. Wrong. Wrong. Wrong. Wrong.

It was the heat AND the humidity.

I tell people that I live in that part of Canada where we are sweltering if the temperature goes above twenty five and frozen if it goes below ten. That statement often confuses my American friends, until I translate the Celsius temperatures into Fahrenheit. It means that I think it's too hot if it is above seventy five and too cold if it's below fifty.

The rest of Canada doesn't really think we should be counted as Canadians because we don't deal with the temperature extremes the people elsewhere the country endure.

I was relieved when that part of my tour ended and I headed for the more moderate temperatures of home, but that global warming puppy must have followed me. It's been well above the aforementioned comfort range ever since I got back.

Because our temperatures spend most of the year in the livable range, air conditioning is not a common feature in our homes. When heat does move in for a couple of weeks we have to get creative.

I've been spending a lot of time in air conditioned stores lately. Some of them sell things I have absolutely no interest in buying -and even less of an idea what they do - but the air is cooler than my apartment. I've been to home improvement stores, even though the only power tool I can use is the telephone. I've ducked into an auto-parts store to cool off, even though the only thing I can say about the operation of my car is that it is green.

I spent a cool and refreshing half-hour looking at in-line skates, even though I walk with crutches clipped to my arms. They had my size, but I couldn't find any that would fit on the bottom of the crutches.

Temperatures like this are dangerous; particularly for husbands; especially those, whose wives have found themselves in that certain, very scary, time of life.

When you are young newlyweds, hot temperatures are not a problem. Your wife will just wear skimpier clothing. This is a good thing.

When your wife is in her fifties and a heat wave hits, she's just as likely to become homicidal, and you are the most likely target of her intended homiciding. This is a bad thing.

My arm brushed against hers in the car yesterday. It scared the heck out of me. I hadn't heard her use that tone of voice since she was in labor and the nurse tried to give her a back rub during a contraction. I think Roman Polanski came up with the idea for the voice of the possessed teenager in Rosemary's Baby, after hearing my wife tell the nurse what she could do with her backrub.

That voice came through loud and clear from my passenger seat.

Until these current heat waves break (the meteorological one and Diane's personal one) I'll be the guy hiding behind the couches at the air conditioned furniture store.

The End Of The Road

It's a sad day.

After six years of faithful service, my car is being forced into retirement. It's like losing a friend.

I've written before about the important features of my car. I can't stress enough how vital they are to the driving experience. Some people might think I'm talking about the engine or some other mechanical feature, and, while I suppose those things are significant, they're nearly not as key to the driving experience as the three features I love about the car.

It's green.

It has a CD player.

It has a sunroof.

Now my green, sunroof-equipped car with a CD player, is on its last legs, or perhaps I should say, on its last wheels.

Last week was not a good week for the car. We left it parked at a hotel in Seattle while we were in Cape Cod. Our plan was to return to Seattle, stay overnight, and drive home in the morning in time for my wife to get to her office by nine o'clock.

While Diane did her hair - a task that all husbands know can take almost as long as driving from Seattle to Vancouver - I started ferrying the luggage to the car. That's when I noticed something missing.

The car keys.

I always keep my car keys inside my computer case when I travel. That way I don't have to fumble with them when I'm going through airport security.

Apparently, airport security fumbled with them.

It seems, the case was dumped as it went through the X-ray equipment, and the keys may still be somewhere inside the machine, under the counter, or inside some other traveler's case.

It should have been a simple task to call a locksmith and get a new key cut, but we had an anti-theft device locked onto the steering wheel.

The fact that it is green, with a CD player and a sunroof, did not seem to help in that situation.

The auto club towed the car to a dealership for me, through Seattle's morning rush hour traffic. After nearly two hours, the car was freed from the anti-theft device and a key was cut.

On the way home a warning light came on. It was an arrow over some waves. My first thought was that I was being advised not to take the car off a cliff into the ocean. After pouring through the owner's manual we determined that it meant that my radiator fluid was low.

It may surprise you – it sure surprised my wife – I was able to open the hood and look at the tank for the radiator fluid. It was full.

"It must be a sensor," I said, trying desperately to sound like I knew what the heck I was talking about.

Obviously, I didn't. The next night the temperature gauge shot up to the top and steam erupted from under the hood. My mechanic, a man who loves to see people like me pull into his parking lot, determined that the water pump was in need of something he called "a ree and ree."

I had no idea what that was, but quickly learned that a ree and ree costs four hundred and forty-seven dollars.

My green, CD and sunroof equipped car has lapped its odometer once and is very close to doing it for a second time. My wife voiced what I already knew but didn't want to think about.

"It's not worth putting any more money into that car," she said. "We're going to have to look for a new one."

I told her I already knew just what to look for in a new car. After thirty-two years of marriage, you'd think she would be prepared, but she thought I was talking about the make and model. When I told her that I thought we should look for a green one with a CD player and a sunroof, she gave me another one of those deer-in-the-headlight looks that I get so often when I open my mouth around here.

The car salesmen we talked to over the weekend did the same thing.

OK, So I Dance To A Different Drummer

Let me say from the outset that I like a broad spectrum of musical styles.

My music collection covers classic rock, current rock, jazz, folk, blues, country and even a bit of classical, although, once you get past the cannon-firing section of the 1812 Overture, my interest wanes quickly. It never makes it as far as opera, which I believe should be classified as cruel and unusual punishment in the civilized world.

Don't tell anyone, but I even like some rap.

I've always considered myself to be bilingual because I can understand English and Bob Dylan.

I enjoy soft quiet music and music that should be played very loud. That said, I still can't understand the people who take all the available cargo space in their cars, and fill it with amplifiers, speakers and more audio technology than Jimi Hendrix could have ever imagined.

I'm convinced that the real purpose of all that technology, is to see if it is possible to blast another car off the road while sitting at a stoplight listening to Led Zeppelin's *Whole Lotta Love*.

I have to admit that the concept of blowing another driver off the road with sound waves intrigues me. I've always wanted a public address system mounted under my hood, so I could loudly point out my feelings toward the drivers who cut me off, or who drive at half the speed limit in the passing lanes of freeways. Every single member of my family has always been quick to say I'm not allowed to get one, for fear I might embarrass them with it.

Loud music in cars has its place. I've been known to use the full potential of my car's stereo system, but only when it has been vitally important to do so.

For example, when my sons were in high school and developed an aversion to public transportation or walking, and they seemed to think that father was a word that was synonymous with chauffeur. They were forever wanting rides to school (a whole three blocks) to their social events, or their after school jobs. Loud music came in handy in my attempts to wean them of that habit.

For some reason, teenage sons were easily mortified by the sight of their father pulling up to the curb to pick them up, with The Eagles, the Beatles or Jimmy Buffet playing at full blast on the car stereo.

It worked even better if I sang along.

One of my sons remains convinced that he will someday have to discuss those events with a therapist.

I was stopped at a traffic light a few days ago, and heard the unmistakable rumble that could only mean a driver with a full payload of audio equipment playing AC/DC was approaching. When the driver stopped beside me, he was clearly fully engulfed in the music. He was playing an imaginary set of drums, and singing at the top of his lungs. As he did, he threw his head back and forward and from side to side in rhythm with the band.

When the thought occurred to me I had been listening to AC/DC well before the other driver was born, I knew I had to retaliate.

I carefully selected the appropriate radio station, and cranked the volume on my stereo to its absolute fullest. I started to wave my arms, dancing in my seat. I even belted out a blues chorus of "Oh baby, baby, baby," as loudly as my larynx would allow.

The other driver stopped pretending to be AC/DC's drummer, and stared at me with one of those wide eyed looks that can only be made if you are in the presence of something extremely unusual. Clearly, my version of what he had been doing seemed very unusual to him.

It might have been the sight of a fifty-something guy behaving the way he had been. It could have been the sheer awe of hearing my blues chorus belting out over his AC/DC.

Or maybe, just maybe, it was the fact that I was doing all that after tuning my radio to the all news station.

Section 2
On The Road Again... And Again

Flying The Not So Friendly Skies

I'm one of those people who would rather be an hour early than a minute late. It's a quality that my wife appreciates, unless it means that she too has to be a hour early with me.

When it comes to traveling, I become particularly stressed at the thought of getting to the airport too late. Now that we live in an era of heightened security, I'm even more concerned with making sure I've lots of time to wait around the airport doing nothing.

There is another reason why I feel the need to get to the airport three or four hours before my flight. No matter how hard I plead, most airlines will not let people book the bulkhead seats in advance.

"They may be needed by someone who is disabled," they always say.

"Do you mean like someone who needs crutches to walk, and has to try to maneuver them, a 6'4" body and legs that don't necessarily do what he wants them to?" I ask.

"Yes, exactly," they say.

"Gee," I say, "that sounds almost exactly like me, so could I please book those seats now."

"No," they say, "those seats can only be booked at the airport."

In other words, "You could just be a big fat liar trying to get one of the only five comfortable seats in the plane."

So I must always arrive at the airport in time to be there when the ticket agents arrive. Without fail, I'm told those seats have already been assigned.

On my flight last week, the seats were occupied by a man suffering a terrible disability. He was flying with his two teenagers.

I, on the other hand, was flying without the deficit teenagers can cause. I had to take my 6'4" body and legs that don't necessarily do what I want them to, and squeeze the whole kit and caboodle into a seat in row seven.

To add insult to potential injury, I was told by the ticket agent that the flight would be delayed, and would not be departing until four hours after its scheduled takeoff. A couple of hours later, after I had already gone through security, I was told that there would be a further three to four hour delay.

What could be a better way to spend a day than having a twelve hour wait for your plane?

Having burning bamboo slivers shoved under your fingernails comes to mind.

At five o'clock in the afternoon, two representatives from the airline came to the gate and announced we would all receive a five-dollar voucher to buy our dinner. Anyone who has ever set foot inside an airport knows just how far five dollars will go in the food service area.

It almost - but not quite - covers a can of soda and a cookie.

You all know me. I'm the sort of person who would just quietly accept the voucher and be done with it, aren't I?

OK, so you do all know me. Of course I didn't sit quietly. Let's just say it's been a long time since I led a good old fashioned insurrection, but it's like riding a bicycle. Once you've done it, it doesn't take long to remember how to do it again.

I loudly said, "What are we supposed to eat for five dollars?"

Cries of, "Yeah, what he said" erupted from around the waiting area.

I demanded to see someone in charge, but she wouldn't venture into the mob, so I had to talk to her on the phone. She told me it was a head office decision. When I asked to talk to the person at their head office, I was told they had left for the day.

I called the number on my ticket. After several attempts, I got someone to make a decision. In the end, we all got a one hundred dollar flight voucher.

They also decided to give us a ten dollar voucher for dinner

It was enough for a diet soda, two cookies and three packs of gum.

I spent the flight throwing gum at the guy with the teenagers in the bulkhead seats.

It made me feel much better.

It's Not A Sport If It Puts Me To Sleep

I seem to be running into sports events a lot on this tour. A couple of weeks ago, I was in San Diego and the city had been invaded by over 20,000 municipal golf course managers from all across the county. Add to that the people who came to town just for the Buick Open Golf Tournament, and you had to be thankful to find a room at the inn.

This past week I was in Saskatoon, Saskatchewan, a city named from the native word for "let's get Lisping Bear to try to say this." With temperatures hovering somewhere between "I think something just snapped off," and "my, that does cause shrinkage, doesn't it?"

I didn't have to worry about too many golfers.

Curlers yes, but not golfers.

Saskatoon was invaded by curling fans, eager to watch the Nokia Briar to determine the Canadian men's champion curling team.

I know I will probably annoy a lot of golf and curling fans, when I say that neither of them strike me as the sort of sports that elicit enough excitement to draw me to watch them, either live or on TV.

I've tried. I really have.

The most exciting part of watching golf on TV for me is trying to determine just how fast the grass is growing on the greens.

And that's only good for a second or two.

Watching someone like Tiger Woods tee off does, I'm sure, have its finer points. Other golfers could probably learn from watching his stance and his swing. It certainly doesn't look anything like my performances with a golf club.

Back before I broke my spine in a serious golfing accident in 1990, I did go out on the links fairly often. I wasn't great, but I could usually break 100.

...on the first nine.

I even have a few accomplishments on the golf course that I'm quite proud of. Other golfers might be satisfied with the occasional birdie or eagle, but I bet even Tiger Woods has never gotten a squirrel on the tenth.

My ball sailed into the branches of a large oak tree and bounced out onto the fairway. At the same time, an unconscious squirrel landed in the rough at the base of the tree.

I once put the ball right onto the green, just inches from the hole. Unfortunately, I was driving into a fairly strong wind and the green I landed on was about fifty feet behind the tee I was driving from. I still say I should have been able to leave a ball marker where the ball stopped, and then use that shot when I eventually made my way around to that hole.

A few moves like those on the PGA circuit could make for a lot better television. I might even be willing to watch if I thought Mike Weir or Vijay Singh had to tee off backwards the way I did.

Curling could also be made a whole lot more interesting for the viewer. I think it probably started out a lot differently. Going back to the origins might make for some excitement. I'll bet that when a few Scots got together to curl for the first time, they had a lot more fun, even if they were standing out on a frozen pond with a Highland gale blowing up their kilts. I can imagine the rules being explained for the first time.

"Aye, Laddie. Here's wha' we're gonna doooooo. We'll paint a bloody big target on the ice at one end of the loch and get a bunch of servants to go oot there and sweep the snow off the ice. Then we'll get us some rocks and hurl them dooone the ice."

"So we'll pitch some wee stones at the target? That doesn't sound like it'd be enough fun to be worth freezin' our sporrans off."

"Nay. Not wee little stones ye daft bugger. I'm talkin' bloody great boulders, and we aim 'em at the servants with the brooms. First one to knock a servant into the target wins."

"Aye. Now yer talkin' aboot a sport, laddie. I'm in."

"Just don't tell the servants beforehand."

If they brought curling back to those origins it might even give Fear Factor a run for its money in the TV ratings.

Especially if they got Donald Trump to fire the first servant.

The Aftermath Of Fear Might Make The Grass Greener

The grass is always greener someplace else - even if you have a septic tank.

We all have images of how nice it must be to live somewhere else. Whenever I'm in San Diego, I wander around thinking, "I could live here." Then I look at the real estate prices and think, "I could never live here."

There is always something about every place, no matter how luxurious it may sound, that makes it a less than desirable place to live. I've seen a lot of that lately.

When I was in Florida a couple of weeks ago, I really enjoyed the warm temperatures and the beaches. It didn't take too long to find some reasons why I wouldn't want to live there, despite the opportunities to sit and write on the beach.

Florida has alligators.

My fear tolerance is such that I get chills just thinking about what it would be like to see a gator dropping by for a visit in my back yard. I can't imagine coming nose to snout with one in a lake. During my ten days in Florida, three people had alligator encounters. That's roughly three too many in my book.

In one case, the pastor of a church near Tampa Bay had to fight off a large alligator in a lake. Why anyone would go swimming in a lake that is known to be inhabited by these beasts is beyond me - even if you are convinced that God is going to protect you.

In fact, if anyone should have known better, it was that particular pastor. The previous pastor of his church had disappeared in that same lake.

Apparently gators think pastors taste a lot like chicken.

I saw a few alligators when I was down there. I was also in several stores that sold alligator and shark teeth. If that's the size of the incisors in the mouths of the local fauna, I think I would just as soon keep a couple of states between me and them.

If you take the frequency of television commercials as a guide, Florida is apparently also overrun with termites. It seemed that every other ad was for a termite removal company. One company advertised that its staff included a termite-sniffing dog. Apparently, dogs can be trained to sniff out termite flatulence.

It comes in pine, cedar and maple scented.

Since dogs can hear such high frequencies, I've to wonder if they can hear it too. Wouldn't that be a nightmare? Can you imagine what it would be like to hear that coming out of the walls twenty-four hours a day?

...and you think cicadas are annoying.

I went to Arizona and Nevada in the winter a few years ago. Naturally, it was sunny and warm. I started thinking about how nice it would be to live there. No snow. No cold rains. No alligators.

Then I saw the snake.

It wasn't just any snake. It was one of those sidewinders. These things just aren't natural. They are looking one way and going another. I've had run-ins with several drivers who tried the same thing.

I'm not ashamed to tell you that snakes are one of the things in this world that can make me scream like a schoolgirl if they get too close to me.

By too close, I mean anywhere within a four state area.

And don't you just hate it when someone tells you not to worry because, "they're more afraid of you than you are of them?"

No sir. That's just not possible. If that thing was more afraid of me than I was of it, then it couldn't have survived the coronary it would have had as soon as it saw me.

Even if we could get St. Patrick to come and drive all of the snakes out of that area so that we could enjoy the sun and the heat, we'd still have the scorpions.

Sitting here at home for a few days before I go out on the next part of the tour, I can relax knowing that I'm not likely to see any alligators or sidewinders.

But I'm still going to check twice when I lift the toilet seat.

We Don't Live In Igloos, Either

As most of you know, I'm a Canadian, eh?

Canada seems to confuse some people.

I spend a lot of time in the United States each year. I can't begin to count the number of people who have wondered if I might know a friend of theirs who lives in Toronto or Montreal. Since those cities are roughly three thousand miles from the part of the country I live in, it is generally pretty unlikely that I will know their Eastern Canadian friends.

The fact that Canada uses the metric system confuses some people. I've written before about the man who told me that he once went to Michigan and thought about crossing over to Canada but wasn't prepared for it. He saw on the news that the temperature was seventy-six in Detroit, but only twenty-four across the river in Windsor. (Seventy-six Fahrenheit and twenty-four Celsius are roughly the same thing.)

I live on the west coast of Canada, roughly one hundred miles north of Seattle. We share similar weather. A lot of people just don't seem to get it. One person who really doesn't get it, and by the number of websites I found that referred to him as a buffoon, doesn't get a lot of things, is baseball commentator Tim McCarver.

(You all thought I was going to say George W. Bush, didn't you?)

In a recent Yankees-Twins baseball playoff game, he pointed out that Twins' rookie first-baseman, Justin Morneau, is from New Westminster, British Columbia. According to McCarver there are moose wandering the streets of New Westminster, and the people there would find fifty-two degrees Fahrenheit "balmy."

I've lived within twenty miles of New Westminster since 1982. In all that time, I can't ever recall a moose walking down Columbia Street or any other of New Westminster's streets for that matter.

The city is mooseless.

It is a moose-free zone.

The moose have vamoosed.

New Westminster is as urban an environment as McCarver's hometown of Memphis. It's a suburb within the metropolitan area of Vancouver, BC. A moose there would be as unusual a sight as a grizzly in Memphis, although Memphis did keep the name 'Grizzlies' for the NBA basketball team it stole from Vancouver.

Fifty-two is about as far from being balmy in New Westminster as it would be in Memphis. Those of us who live in this area are not really considered to be true Canadians because we rarely see snow. In the past hundred years there have only been seven white Christmases here.

Like the rest of the Pacific Northwest, we like our natural environment. It always amazes me how, when some people just don't get that, they really don't get it.

The major daily newspaper in my area ran a letter to the editor recently, from a tourist who had visited the Northwest from Spain. He clearly didn't get it.

He wrote that his visit here had been spoiled by an overabundance of trees.

He could not see the rivers from the road because there were too many trees in the way. He could not see the ocean from another highway because, once again, those nasty trees got in the way.

Everywhere he looked he saw trees. He didn't want to see trees. He wanted to see scenery as he drove along our highways, and he felt he should let us know that in order to do that, we should cut down those trees that are in the way.

What the tree-hating Spaniard didn't realize is that those trees are part of the scenery here in the Northwest, and they provide homes for birds and animals.

As the old saying goes, bears crap in the woods. If there weren't trees, they'd have to hold it. I don't think any Spanish tourist is physically or psychologically equipped to deal with a constipated grizzly.

If those trees weren't there, the grizzly bears and cougars would be out along the roadsides, waiting to prey on Spanish tourists who get lured into a false sense of security by the sight of rivers and oceans. The trees are there for their protection. They should be thankful.

Without them, they might even get trampled by a moose in downtown New Westminster.

They Could Have Asked

It may be true you can't go home again, but it is still possible to take a drive past for old times sake.

While in Ontario on this part of my book tour, I've driven past several of the places I called home between 1953 and 1982. It's been a trip filled with nostalgia for a time long ago and far away.

Of all of the houses that have been part of my married life, one stands out above all the rest as my absolute favorite. It was an old farmhouse, nestled on three acres of land, five miles from the nearest paved road. It had been built in the 1890's and stood beside a barn and a garage of similar vintage.

On my last visit to the area five years ago, the house looked much as it did when Diane and I lived there. The only real change was the size of the trees that we had planted as seedlings around the property. They were now the tall pines and spruce trees I had envisioned, protecting the property from the winter winds that buffeted the house as they bore down on it across open fields each year.

It had been our second anniversary present to each other. We're now getting close to our thirty-third.

It was our place of refuge from our jobs in the city, forty miles away. Each night we would leave our work behind and return to the house. We tended a one-acre vegetable garden, shared the space with our dogs and cats, and basked in the blissful silence of the country life.

In the winter months, heat leaking from the house provided warmth for a pack of wolves that would sleep beside the kitchen wall, returning to the woods at the first sounds of movement inside the house each morning, and leaving only the indentations their bodies made in the snow beside the house as evidence of their visits.

As I approached Ottawa for an appearance last week, I turned off the highway and headed down the back road that would take me to that house. A few new houses had popped up along the road, but the familiar pothole-ridden gravel track tested the shock absorbers of my rental car, the way I remembered it doing to my own vehicles in the mid-1970's.

The house came into sight a mile before I reached it. Even from that distance I could tell that something was horribly wrong.

The barn, which once proudly showed its age by its weathered gray boards, was now a bright white. I hate to imagine how many gallons of paint those boards had absorbed to bring it to the blinding white building that looked very little like the one my memories portrayed.

As I neared the laneway, I could see the house was no longer the way I remembered it, either. Someone had built a huge addition onto the back and added a covered veranda that wrapped itself around two sides of the building.

It looked surprisingly like the image of the plans Diane and I had for that house if we could have ever saved enough money to have the work done.

I only stopped for a minute to look at it. Had the situation been different, I might have pulled in the laneway for a better look and a chance to refresh my memories of the place. But with all of the changes that had been made, I just couldn't bring myself to do it. I took one last look at it in my rearview mirror before turning the corner and heading back toward the highway.

I was a little surprised to find that I was feeling angry about what I had just seen. I suppose it might be understandable to be a little angry with myself for selling the best house we would ever own, but my annoyance wasn't directed at myself. I was ticked off with the people who now owned the property and who had made those changes I would have liked to have made for myself.

It's not because they did it.

It's just that they didn't even bother to get my permission first.

Am I Being Served?

I'm beginning to have my doubts about the service in service industries.

I may not be the best one to comment, because in the years that I spent as a Canadian civil servant I did my best to avoid serving.

And I was rarely civil.

Still, comment I must, because of a couple of recent experiences with the so-called service industry sector that were definitely lacking in the service department.

I was speaking at a conference in Philadelphia several weeks ago. The conference organizers were paying for my accommodations. Still, the hotel wanted an imprint of my credit card in case I charged anything to the room. When I left the hotel I owed them $13.64 for telephone calls. I signed a receipt for that amount.

For some reason the hotel put $454.89 on my credit card.

The ripple effect was incredible. As I was nearing the end of a three-week leg of my book tour, the additional charge put my credit card slightly into overdraft. That's when the militant banking wing of the service sector got into the act.

They called my home in the evening and left word that I was in trouble with them. My wife really appreciated getting that call after a long day's work, so she sent me an email telling me to call the credit card company.

Now, it may have been evening on the west coast, but it was heading for midnight where I was on the east coast. I, too, was thrilled by the news.

When I called the company, I was able to quickly determine what had caused the problem, but quickly discovered I had another problem. Credit card employees are not inclined to believe that problems of this type are not the customer's fault. I was told it was my problem and I had better get it fixed quickly, lest I face the greater wrath of the credit department.

When I asked the woman how I was supposed to get it fixed, she simply – and not too subtly – let me know that I would have to figure it out by myself.

Much to everyone's surprise, I managed to do just that. It only took me until four o'clock in the morning. I finally arranged a conference call between the hotel's night manager and the credit card company.

Amazingly, before hanging up, both of them asked if there was anything else they could do to serve me.

I think I had been serviced enough for one day.

This week, I tried to use a courier company to get one piece of paper to my wife's office at home, from Memphis, where I was doing an appearance.

I asked the clerk to use Fed-Ex, because I can normally trust them, and because everything Fed-Ex ships eventually has to go through Memphis anyway. The clerk said he found UPS better at getting overnight deliveries to Canada.

I must have misheard him. I'm now convinced that he must have said that UPS was better at fouling up a delivery to Canada. Someone in the brain trust of UPS decided that a letter to Canada must be accompanied by an invoice for the contents.

I suppose I could have written an invoice to my wife for the value of the piece of paper that was in the envelope.

It took twelve telephone calls, each one requiring an complete explanation of the problem from scratch, to get the letter delivered. In one call, I was told the people who could answer my problem didn't come to work until six o'clock in the evening.

In another call, I discovered that UPS did not keep a record of the previous calls by the waybill number of the package. They recorded everything by the telephone number you gave them. Over the course of my conversations with them, I drove from Memphis to St. Louis. I didn't keep a record of the phone number I had used in Memphis.

It's probably just as well I dealt with the UPS people by telephone. If I had been face-to-face with them I think I would have found a way to give them another reason for their shorts to be brown.

Traveling Lighter

I spent the weekend in Casper, Wyoming. My luggage decided to extend its stay there even longer.

Getting to Casper is an experience in itself. I drove from my home near Vancouver, BC to Seattle to catch the plane. It's a three hour drive, depending on whether there is a strip search involved at the border. It's worth it, because there is several hundred dollars difference between flying from Seattle compared with Vancouver.

Perhaps Canadian airlines were trying to discourage me from going to Casper.

Perhaps I should have listened.

I had to change planes in Denver. I always find it odd getting off a plane in Denver. It looks like the pilot accidentally parked at a shopping mall instead of an airport. I think there are more stores in the Denver airport than in the little town I call home.

I knew I was in trouble when I saw the plane for the flight to Casper. I've seen bigger SUV limos in Las Vegas. I think it was built to serve a number of purposes. Getting passengers comfortably to Casper, Wyoming is fairly well down the list in terms of priority. I think we might have done a couple of crop dusting passes before our final approach.

I think Rancher Bob was in the jump seat looking for a few head of lost cattle.

As I headed to the baggage claim area I could see my hotel's courtesy shuttle sitting right outside. I was thankful it wasn't a covered wagon with a couple of head of oxen pulling it.

Of course, in the two minutes it took to pick up my bag, the driver headed off into the high prairie. After forty minutes of trying to reach the hotel, I finally found out that it was entirely my fault. I hadn't spoken slowly enough, when I told the hotel reservations clerk that I needed a ride from the airport.

The van showed up a half hour later. By this point, I had already been in transit for seventeen hours. I was looking forward to collapsing into the bed. Apparently, that would be delayed a bit further. The kid who drove the van disappeared into the airport for a half hour. He came out to tell me that we would be waiting for the next passenger plane/crop duster/cattle search and rescue plane to arrive.

Then he disappeared again.

It was well after dark, so they must have been having trouble seeing the field that needed crop dusting, or the lost cattle. The flight was over an hour late.

I have to admit, my time on the ground in Casper was quite enjoyable. I spoke at the Wyoming Writers' Conference, and they were a great audience. I did feel a little out of place though. With what remained of the tan I got in Florida last month, I was the closest thing to a person of color in Casper.

Casper The Friendly Ghost is darker than Casper, Wyoming.

Casper is just shy of a mile above sea level. I live at about thirty feet above sea level depending on what the tide is like. I never knew that just trying to breathe could be considered an aerobic exercise. I thought that would be the only problem I'd have with the thin air.

Unh-unh... Nope... Not even close... Remember the passenger plane/crop duster/cattle search and rescue planes? They can't take off with a full load in the thin air when the temperature goes above ninety.

Two things you can be sure of in that situation: 1) it will be over ninety when I have to leave, and 2) the airline will have sold every seat on the flight, even though they know that the odds are pretty good it will be over ninety in Casper in June.

Five people had to be convinced to spend more time in Casper, and none of the luggage belonging to the rest of us would be loaded onto the plane.

So, here I'm in Washington, DC, about to be honored at an event at the National Press Club, and my suit, dress shoes, and razor, are still in Casper, Wyoming.

...but there is some good news – I think Ranger Bob found his cows on the flight out.

From Bucksnort To Peculiar And Points In Between

Traveling as much as I do on book promotion tours shows me a great variety of signs I wouldn't normally see. Between April 16th and May 14th, I only slept in my own bed for two nights. The rest of the time was on the road in Ontario, Oklahoma, Arkansas, Tennessee, Missouri, Illinois, and Indiana.

Some of those sights really left me wondering. For some reason, a great many of them are along I-40 and the surrounding area between Oklahoma City and Nashville.

About fifty miles east of Jackson, Tennessee, there is a large billboard encouraging travelers to visit the Patsy Cline crash sight. Cline was killed in a plane crash in Foggy Bottom, near Camden, Tennessee in 1963.

Apparently, each year, thousands of people stop by to see the place where her song *I Fall To Pieces* became somewhat prophetic.

I decided to not be one of them.

A little closer to Nashville, between Only, TN and Spot, TN (I'm not kidding, these are real places) is a place called Bucksnort.

Bucksnort is not by any means a large metropolis. Truth be known, it's the kind of place that would cause Rand to turn to McNally and say, "Where?"

I wasn't sure if that was the price of cocaine or snuff back when the town was established, so I checked the internet to see if there was a logical reason for naming a town Bucksnort. I assumed it would have had something to do with a local resident being startled by the noise made by a large male deer.

I assumed wrong.

The answer I found was almost as odd as the name itself. Apparently, Bucksnort is named for William ("Buck") Pamplin, who owned the land prior to the Civil War.

The information on a website established by his descendents says, "William loved whiskey. He would get soused to the ears with the sweet, smelly stuff, and when he did, he would roar and snort till everyone around heard him. They would say: 'Just listen to Buck snort.' His snorting became so frequent and the comment was made so often, that the neighbors soon found themselves running the last two words together, thus the place was called Bucksnort."

On this same trip I was invited to do an appearance in Poteau, Oklahoma, where I discovered it to be the home of the world's highest hill. I'm sure you'll all want to rush right down there to see it.

The summit of Canaval Hill is at an elevation of 1,999 feet, making it just one foot shy of the required two-thousand feet to have it officially declared a mountain.

While I was there I found, an even more intriguing sign than the one designating the world's tallest hill. Poteau is also home to the Pansy Kidd Middle School.

Obviously, it has been named for someone named Pansy Kidd, but I can't imagine any guy, no matter how secure he might be in his manhood, wanting to admit that he attended that school.

I don't care how you spell it; it's still going to sound like you went to a school for pansy kids.

A little to the southeast of Poteau is what remains of the town of Ink, Arkansas. Ink hasn't been an official town since it lost its post office in 1967, but the story of its name is a marvelous bit of folklore.

In the late 1800's, the residents petitioned the government for a post office. A local schoolteacher solicited suggestions on written ballots bearing the words, "Write in ink." Apparently people took the instructions a little too literally and wrote in "Ink."

Closer to Little Rock is a town that just sounds unsanitary, and the likely home of a lot of people suffering from warty tongues. Toad Suck Ferry, Arkansas is probably a good place to avoid opening a restaurant.

Perhaps the oddest town sign I saw along the way was between Kansas City and Springfield, Missouri. It sounds like my sort of place. It has a name that fits my outlook on life and describes how a lot of people think of me.

Perhaps I should move to Peculiar, Missouri.

Oh Canada, You're Calling Your Town What?

I received an email telling me that last week's column containing references to some odd signs and town names I had seen on my travels through the American Mid-South, was not appreciated.

"Canadians like you shouldn't make fun of Americans," was one of the more polite comments in the note. Others could not be reprinted in mainstream newspapers.

America is not the only place where there are odd names and signs. Over the years, I've run into quite a few north of the forty-ninth parallel, as well. In an effort to placate my disgruntled reader, who proved to be very well versed in the use of a vocabulary that would make a longshoreman blush, I will dedicate this column to odd Canadian place names.

Just a few miles east of my home is what is left of the town of Spuzzum, British Columbia. Whenever I would pass through it on the highway, its name reminded me of an unpleasant bodily fluid. I've always wondered if, during its heyday in the gold rush years of the nineteenth century, there was a big market for spittoons in Spuzzum.

On a similar note, BC is also home to the town of Yahk. While I don't know the history of how the town got its name, it sounds like the kind of noise a prospector might make, coughing up some Spuzzum in the middle of the winter on the British Columbia/Idaho/Montana border.

Canadians seem to have used body parts to name certain towns and geographical landmarks. There is Crotch Lake in Ontario, Fanny Bay in British Columbia, Joe Betts Arm in Newfoundland, and Head Smashed In, Alberta. The last one is a cliff the Blackfoot would chase herds of buffalo over in a rather effective hunting system.

I was disappointed to learn that Tete Jaune, BC was French for Yellow Head, and not a reference to Jaune's feminine features.

I'm not sure if the residents of Vulcan, Alberta have pointy ears, but not far away, in St. Paul, Alberta, the town leaders felt it necessary to build a flying saucer landing pad as their project to mark Canada's centennial in 1967.

Coincidence? I don't think so.

This column runs in the newspaper in Saskatoon, Saskatchewan. While not a particularly funny name, it has often confused people visiting from other parts of the world.

An old Bob Hope movie has a scene in which his character asks where he is and is told "Saskatoon, Saskatchewan."

When another character asks him what he found out, he said, "I don't know. They don't speak English here."

I'm not sure how a town could get a name like Ecum Secum, Nova Scotia, but it must be quite a place. When I checked online to see if I could learn anything about the town, I found there is a dating service specifically for the residents of Ecum Secum, including listings for both straight and gay residents.

A little south of Ecum Secum, is Musquodoboit Harbour. One can only assume that it is an area infested with blood-sucking insects.

Language changes over time, and I've to wonder if that's why some town names sound odd to us today. Perhaps at the time the good townsfolk of the area chose the name it was considered perfectly acceptable. Then again, perhaps they knew they could raise more than a few eyebrows with town names like Kinmount, Ontario.

Newfoundland is home to a wide variety of town names that all seem to have a certain theme to them. I will leave you to your own imagination as to how the towns of Dildo, Come By Chance and Conception Bay got their names. There are several even more graphic names that I will let you look up on your own on the Newfoundland map.

So, while driving past a place like Bucksnort, Tennessee, gives me a laugh along the road, it is not just my American friends that I'm lambasting over their town name selections. My country can match the USA any day in picking questionable names.

Still, you have to admit, Dildo, Newfoundland does have a nice buzz to it, don't you think?

I'm An In-Flight Insecurity Risk

When you spend as much time on airplanes as I do, you start to feel pretty good about the improved security measures. As a frequent flyer, I can tell you that the last thing I want is to have my flight interrupted by a sudden cabin depressurization, because someone came on board with a bomb hidden in their support hose.

Over the last few years, we, the traveling public, have all had to deal with a little more preflight inconvenience to decrease the chances of in-flight terrorist activities.

I'm good with that.

As most of my regular readers know, I find it difficult to refrain from commenting on most subjects that strike me as odd, unusual, or just plain dumb. There is a line I will not cross, though.

I don't joke with airport security about bombs, terrorists, or anything remotely security related. I've witnessed what can happen to a person who makes that mistake.

It wasn't pretty.

The man was taken to a room somewhere in the bowels of the airport and for all I know he may still be there.

As I said, I won't cross that line, but I will point out to the security personnel, when they have asked me a question that is just plain dumb.

Every single security agent, at every airport and for every flight I've taken in the past several years, has asked me the same question. It is so blatantly inane that it does not qualify for a straight answer in my book.

Pointing to the crutches that are fastened to my forearms, they look at me with all seriousness and ask, "Do you need those to walk with?"

"No," I reply, "I'm making a fashion statement. Someday everyone is going to walk around on these things just for the sheer enjoyment they bring."

I realize they are aware the metal detector is going to detect I'm carrying two large pieces of metal through it. I suppose an alternative would be to have the security agent carry me through.

Not one of them has ever seemed the slightest bit interested in doing that.

Just recently, on a flight from Vancouver, BC to Las Vegas, I encountered a new FAA regulation designed to prevent midair terrorist attacks, make my life miserable, and strike fear into the hearts of at least fifty of my fellow passengers.

I qualify for the disabled seating position, which is generally in the first row of the main cabin immediately behind the first class section. On a 737-400 there is a lavatory at the front of the aircraft six rows ahead of me and two at the back, some twenty-five rows behind me.

The FAA has decreed that on international flights, no one from the main cabin may use the lavatory at the front of the aircraft. Therefore, instead of ten first class aisle-seat passengers worrying that a bit of turbulence might make me land in their laps, nearly fifty main cabin aisle-seat passengers watch me try to make the trek down the aisle toward them; an aisle that is, by the way, clearly too narrow to allow my crutches to provide full or even adequate stability.

I think the majority of those poor people, who can easily imagine me crash landing on top of them, do not believe the FAA's new rule has heightened their personal security.

Flight attendants tell me that having me walk the length of the plane at least once in every flight, significantly increases the subsequent alcohol consumption of the passengers seated between me and the lavatory.

Quite frankly, I don't feel all that secure either, even if I make it all the way to the end of the plane without crashing. When I get there, I've to try to wedge myself and my crutches between the baby changing table, the sink, and the doorway in a one-size-fits-all lavatory designed, I'm sure, by the same guy who designed one-size-fits-all hospital gowns.

But that's another story, and one that might make you wake up screaming in the night, should the image of me in that situation invade your subconscious.

One Man's Finger Is Another's Bait

Every time I head out on the road for an appearance tour, I know somewhere along the way I'm going to discover new things and perhaps even learn a thing or two.

This trip has certainly been educational.

I realize we all have different ways of doing things, and we even have different names for doing the same things, so I often find myself needing to ask for information about something I hear or see along the way.

Shortly after arriving in Oklahoma City last week, I heard a news report about a project that involved stocking a river in the city with catfish. The report advised listeners they would be allowed to use a rod and reel to try to catch the fish, but that noodling was not allowed.

Noodling?

I immediately came to the conclusion that anglers in Oklahoma used pasta as bait, and for some reason, this was not going to be allowed in the quest for these particular catfish.

It made me wonder just what type of pasta might work best. I suppose linguine could be disguised to look like a worm. Perhaps those bowtie-shaped noodles might make an interesting lure. Ravioli and lasagna noodles both struck me as being too large for catfish, but they might be useful if someone went deep-sea noodling.

As reasonable as my assumption about noodling might have been, it should be no surprise to any of my readers that I was off track.

Way, way off track.

When I asked someone about the practice of fishing with pasta, I learned the true meaning of noodling. Pasta is not involved in any shape or way. I almost wish it were. Learning the true definition of catfish noodling was more than a little bit disturbing.

A noodler puts his bare hand into the water and wiggles it around under logs or rocks where a large catfish may be lurking. The catfish will grab the finger and the fight is on.

Apparently, catfish can grow to weights approaching one hundred pounds, therefore, noodlers must be quite strong.

Inexperienced noodlers are advised to noodle with a buddy, which sounds dirty when you say it out loud.

More than a few noodlers have drowned while partaking in this activity. No matter what Ernest Hemmingway might have said, no fish is worth dying for.

The more I looked into the practice of noodling, the more I became aware it was not something I would be willing to try. Somehow using my body parts as bait didn't have much appeal.

One man was more than willing to show me his noodling scars as he explained the hazards involved.

Catfish have very strong jaws and teeth like rough sandpaper, which accounted for several of his wounds. They also have those sharp spines coming out of their faces that can puncture skin.

He pointed out that catfish are not the only creatures that lurk under logs or rocks in the water. He was particularly proud of one large scar on his upper arm. It was the result of noodling a beaver. He added that snapping turtles are best to be avoided.

Ya think?

While I had determined there was very little chance that I would ever let myself get talked into noodling, one final hazard put the icing on the cake. Apparently, it is not all that uncommon for a noodler to find that the log he is wiggling his fingers around, does not house a catfish, a beaver, or a snapping turtle. It could just as easily be the home of a water moccasin.

I avoid snakes with my undivided attention. I'm even secure enough in my manhood to admit that if I ever came anywhere near a water moccasin, I would most likely scream like a little girl.

And that would be after I stopped screaming at a pitch that only dogs could hear.

The fact that there is the remotest possibility of a water moccasin being in the same river would keep me out of the water.

So no matter how hungry I might ever be, you are not going to catch me noodling.

With or without a buddy.

Being Canadian Means Never Having To Say You're British

As a Canadian who spends a great deal of time in the United States, I realize there are things that confuse my southern neighbors about my homeland. Perhaps it is the responsibility of people like me to educate Americans about their big old friendly neighbor. On the other hand, there are probably a lot of Canadians who would just as soon I didn't try, because they are afraid that Americans might get the wrong idea about Canada from my view of things. Still, many Americans turn to me for information about the Great White North. I usually hear the same questions whenever I do an appearance south of the 49th parallel.

Americans all seem to think we Canadians say "oot" or "aboot" instead of "out or about." There are over 30 million people in Canada. I've never heard any of the ones I've met say "oot" or "aboot."

Many Americans wonder what I see is the biggest difference between our two countries. All in all, we are pretty similar. We Canadians just aren't nearly as well armed as Americans. I can only think of one person I know who owns a gun, and he's a cop. That same situation seems to go all the way through our culture to include our military forces. The amusement park at the West Edmonton Mall has more submarines than our navy.

You need to look no further than the newspapers in both countries last week, to see this difference. The front page of a couple of American newspapers I read featured stories about the war with Iraq, a couple of murders, and a few armed holdups. On the same day, and on just about any other day for the past year or so, we've been dealing with the greatest outrage of them all: The National Hockey League strike/lockout.

Citizens of states close to the border know more about us up here, but even they have questions about us. Some that I often hear are about our money.

While every American bill is the same color, our five is blue, our ten is purple, our twenty is green, and our fifty is orange. I think our hundred is brown, but hey, I'm a writer. I don't get to see them all that often. When Americans ask about this, I explain that our multi-colored currency is actually a protection against money laundering. Criminals avoid laundering our money because with so many colors they'd have to do too many separate loads.

Americans also often wonder, "If Canada isn't part of Britain, why is the Queen on your money?"

Frankly, I don't have a satisfactory answer for that one. Canadians have been self-governed since 1867. Still, we keep the matriarch of the world's most famous dysfunctional family on our coins, twenty-dollar bills, and stamps. (That statement should get the mail from raging monarchists flowing to the Canadian papers that carry my column.)

Lizzie the Second tours Canada every so often so that she can show us she really does relate well with her Canadian subjects. On one of her recent trips, she took time out to drop the puck for the opening face-off for a Vancouver Canucks' NHL preseason game. I watched the ceremony, but I've to tell you I was quite disappointed in the whole thing. They gave the woman a carpet to walk on. I think if she was going to be allowed to disrupt something as important as the opening face-off of a hockey game, she should have been wearing skates.

A tour by the Queen won't do a whole lot for Canada's image as a unique entity. The American networks all covered her puck dropping. As a result, I had to answer all the same questions again, the next time I went to the States.

No, Tony Blair is not Paul Martin's boss.

No, tea is not our national drink, but it's almost the same color as our real national drink. The easy way to tell the difference is that tea doesn't form a white head when you pour it out of a bottle.

And no, the guy on our ten-dollar bill isn't Prince Philip on a bad hair day.

Luggage: The New In-Flight Terror

Airplanes seem to give me a lot of material. I spend so much time in them I might as well start using a 737 as my mailing address.

Last year I bought a new suitcase. I have a certain expectation about the expected longevity of a piece of luggage, probably based on my father's suitcase that he used from the 1920's to the 1970's. My one-year-old suitcase looks like it has been used as an armament tote in Baghdad.

After the insurgents blew it up.

Airline baggage handlers have all but destroyed it. My wife does not want to be seen with me and that piece luggage.

Perhaps if I tried using it as a carry-on piece, I could get a few more months out of it. It is somewhat over the legal size for carry-on luggage, but that would just make me fit in with so many other passengers. On my last flight, I swear I saw more oversized luggage being carried onto the plane by passengers, than was being stuffed, slammed, and dropkicked into the cargo hold by the baggage handlers.

Over the past couple of years, I've come to the conclusion there is an FAA regulation that at least three passengers are required to slam me in the side of the head with their carry-on luggage before every flight. They, or perhaps second-string luggage slammers, are then required to repeat the process on their way off the plane.

Nothing can strike fear into my heart faster than seeing an oversized woman carrying an oversized backpack down the aisle towards me.

What truly amazes me, is that the people carrying backpacks seem to have absolutely no idea they have eighteen extra inches sticking out behind them. When they turn their body, the backpack swings into the head of the closest passenger – apparently, that usually means me.

On my flight from Denver to Chicago last week, a woman brought a red suitcase on board that was easily fifty percent bigger than the maximum carry-on dimensions. She tried her best to stuff it into an overhead bin. When that didn't work, she simply left it teetering over the seats below, while she went to find her own seat, several rows back.

The flight attendants were left to try to make it fit. They managed to get the bin closed, but I was convinced that the door was going to blow off at the slightest provocation.

On another recent flight, a man whose seat was in the row ahead of me and across the aisle, put a large briefcase and a carry-on bag in the bin over my head. He had to move my briefcase to get his in, but it was clearly more important for him to get his stuff stuffed into the bin than for me to have access to my case.

When he finished jamming his cases into the bin, he wedged a large note pad into the front of the bin and slammed the door. It wasn't any simple run-of-the-mill note pad. It was leather-covered with large gold corner protectors. The note pad I carry is about three-quarters of an inch thick. This one was easily two to three times that size.

It was a fairly turbulent flight. When we arrived at our destination the owner of all that luggage over my head was the first to his feet. When he opened the overhead bin, the notepad tumbled out, hitting me in the forehead.

The man was obviously concerned. He carefully examined the note pad to make sure it hadn't sustained any damage. I'm sure he was quite thankful it hadn't gotten any of my blood on it. Without a word, he deplaned, while the flight attendants brought me a bag of ice.

Carry-on luggage clearly has three purposes: preventing it from taking a side trip to New Delhi instead of flying with you to New York; avoiding waiting for the baggage handlers to deal with it when you get to your destination; and, perhaps most importantly, causing me to wonder whether I will survive the next luggage landslide or backpack pummeling.

I think I'm going to start wearing a helmet.

Sign Language

I've gotten used to the fact we have so many different accents in North America. It can be a chore to try to understand what we are saying to one another. I think I've mastered the Deep South, and the Midwest, but I still have people telling me that I talk funny because of the way my Canadian accent pronounces out, about and house.

My tour hit New England this week and I'm faced with trying to decipher an entirely new dialect.

I was sitting in the parking lot of a shopping center on Cape Cod trying to determine where I was on the road map, while my wife tried to confuse the clerks in the store by asking for pop instead of soda. I finally realized it was time to swallow my male pride and ask a local for directions.

I didn't expect his answer to border on the obscene, and in fact it did not. It jumped right into the middle of the obscene.

"Well," he said, "ya need ta skip the first fork in the road and take the second fork."

That doesn't sound all that bad when I write it in plain old everyday English, but you have to understand that the way he said the word "*fork*" did not sound anything like the implement you wrap spaghetti around.

He dropped the *r* and the *o* took on the sound of a *u*.

For obvious reasons, I can't include the phonetic spelling of the way he said fork in a column that runs in mainstream newspapers, but you all know the word I mean.

It made the directions sound like the kind of advice a father would give his son, as in, "Don't take the first..."

I can accept the fact that we all say things a little differently, but I still expect that road signs should be pretty much the same everywhere. Up until now, my experience has been able to confirm that thesis. *Stop*, *One Way*, and *Slow Men At Work* are universally understood throughout North America, although I've often wondered why those slow workmen are still able to keep their jobs.

Of course, *End Road Work* has always made me think that it is someone's idea of a protest sign against highway expansion projects.

Coming to Cape Cod has brought me face-to-face with some road signs that have left me wondering if I haven't been somehow transported to another continent, planet, or some really strange parallel universe.

Take for example *Thickly Settled 30 MPH*.

That sign appears every few hundred feet along the winding back roads around the Cape.

My first thought was that the residents who settled there were a bit thick.

Perhaps, there was a feeling that anyone who would settle on the sandy desolate shores of the Upper Cape must have to been a bit thick to choose that location over other more verdant locations along the coast. Today, anyone who would pay the real estate prices for a home on Cape Cod would have to be a bit thick.

Perhaps *Thickly Settled* refers to the dimensions of the current settlers. Just after passing one of the signs I saw a woman in a bright purple house dress whose "thickly" had settled so far, it was nearly dragging on the ground.

While the rest of the road building industry has long ago eliminated traffic circles from the landscape, they are still quite common in Cape Cod. Except the folks in Cape Cod do not call it a traffic circle. It's a rotary.

My wife, a member of the militant provisional wing of Rotary International, finds that quite amusing. She wants a picture of the sign found a hundred feet ahead of every one of these traffic abominations.

"*Yield To Cars In Rotary.*"

It makes me a bit nervous about letting her drive our rental car. I can almost picture her driving headlong into the flow around a traffic circle, screaming out the window, "Get out of my way. I'm a Rotarian!"

The image is more than a bit frightening. If it came to pass it would undoubtedly make the rest of the drivers head for the first fork in the road.

No matter how they pronounce it.

A Hex On Massachusetts Drivers

I spent two days in Boston. Frankly, it's a wonder I've any hair left.

Boston drivers are a unique sort. I'm not sure what befalls the typical friendly New Englander when they get behind the wheel of a car, but it's not pretty.

Someone many years ago, probably a demented high school driver's education teacher who lost all remnants of his sanity in an unfortunate parallel parking incident, started teaching Massachusetts drivers how to behave behind the wheel. It's been all downhill since then.

In the Boston area, stop signs do not necessarily mean stop. In fact, I think they should take the word *STOP* off of them altogether. In its place, on every red octagon in the state, put the word CHICKEN.

That's the game they all play when they come to a stop sign.

Driving down the road believing you have the right of way to proceed because the other streets have stop signs when they intersect with the one you are on, is an accident waiting to happen. Any car approaching your street will race to the stop and poke as far out into the intersection as its driver dares, just to see if you swerve, offer to let them out ahead of you, or soil yourself.

On a number of occasions, I thought I might have done the latter, partially because of the drivers of the other cars, and partially because of my wife shouting, "I don't think he's planning on stopping."

In one particularly bad five-mile stretch of road, she gasped so many times because of the other drivers, I thought she might hyperventilate.

A left side turn signal blinking in Boston does not necessarily mean the driver is planning to make a left turn anytime in the foreseeable century. It could very well be that the signal was engaged when he purchased the car and he has never bothered to turn it off.

It could also mean he his planning on turning right across three lanes of traffic and onto a freeway off-ramp directly in front of you.

That's just another way for Bostonians to enjoy the pastime of making unwary tourists stain the upholstery of their rental cars.

Boston is one of America's oldest cities. Therefore, many of its roads were designed in the early part of the eighteenth century, with no forethought for the day in the twenty-first century that Bostonians would no longer be dependent on horses. Still, that should not have caused the kinds of problems that Boston drivers present to unwary tourists.

We tried to find The Old North Church, where lanterns were hung signaling Paul Revere to go madly riding through the countryside, announcing that the British were heading towards Concord and Lexington at the beginning of the Revolutionary War.

Paul Revere had it easy. He didn't have to deal with Boston drivers.

As we drove up the hill toward the church, we noticed something unusual. The street was lined with parked cars. Beside many of them were second cars, abandoned by their drivers who had gone into the shops along the street. Trying to make your way along the road without hitting oncoming traffic, which was also trying to avoid double parked cars on its side of the road, or running over pedestrians – a group only slightly less annoying than the drivers - was enough to make me want to pull my hair out by the roots.

A big part of that problem was the total lack of anyplace to park more than one or two cars anywhere in the city. We drove to Salem with the plan to take a tour of the witch trial locations. The tour was an hour-and-a-half long. The only parking we found in the area was limited to thirty minutes. On any other day, and in any other location, I might have been willing to risk getting a parking ticket.

Salem being Salem, I was afraid I would come back to my car and find that instead of a ticket, a coven of meter maids would have turned it into a pumpkin.

I don't think the car rental company would have appreciated that.

Brotherly Love

I had a rather unique introduction to Philadelphia – *The City of Brotherly Love* - when I arrived there last week. It made me remember that even in the case of city slogans, old or new, there is not always truth in advertising. Philadelphia's new slogan is: *The City That Loves You Back*.

Neither of them seemed to fit with the response I received from the first person I spoke to there.

I managed to get myself lost in downtown Philadelphia. No matter what way I turned, I could not find my hotel. I had the address, and it seemed to be a fairly straightforward location to find on the map. It probably would have been if downtown Philadelphia wasn't filled with one-way streets – all seeming to run in the opposite direction than I needed to go.

Of course, it didn't help that my hotel had a sign that could only be seen once you had actually arrived at the hotel, so I never knew whether or not I was getting any closer to the place.

For forty-five minutes, I circled around looking for the place. That's usually the point when I'm willing to let my guard down, throw my male pride out the window, and ask for directions.

Oh, the shame of it all.

Even that wasn't going to be as easy as it sounds. In all my travels around the core of Philadelphia, I hadn't seen a gas station or an available parking spot.

Finally, an opportunity presented itself. I pulled up at a red light beside a police officer in an SUV. It's always been my experience, that police officers in SUV's are further up the totem pole than the ones driving around in sedans. I just knew that here, in world famous City of Brotherly Love, he was just the right person to ask for directions to my hotel.

His answer was direct, to the point, short, but lacking in the brotherly love department.

"What do I look like, a tour guide?"

Actually, he had an adjective in front of 'tour guide,' but my editors don't let me use that word in my column.

I said, "No, but my mommy always told me that if I was lost I should ask a policeman for help."

The look I got back didn't seem to be filled with brotherly love.

I had been thinking about brotherly love earlier in the week, too. On my way north from Washington, DC, I decided to take the longer route and pay a visit to Gettysburg. It had been almost forty years since I had been there.

As a child, I visited a lot of Civil War battlegrounds. My mother had been very interested in the history of that period, which meant our spring breaks were spent touring battlefields - Gettysburg, Manassas, Antietam, Fredricksburg...

Basically, if a Union soldier pointed his gun out the window at a Confederate soldier across the street, I've been to that battle site.

Despite being a somewhat disinterested ten or eleven-year-old visiting those sites, the seeds of interest were planted, and I found I had a desire to see them again.

It took me over three hours to see it all. In all that time, I was more often alone than with other visitors. Early June was obviously a good time to visit, because it fell after most of the school groups had visited, and before parents started bringing their children there for an educational vacation.

I remembered the stories about brothers fighting there for the opposite sides. As I stood alone, looking over the boulders that littered the side of Little Round Top, the hill that was the scene of the decisive part of the battle, I thought about what it would have been like to see my brother coming up the hill. A lot fewer men would have died at Gettysburg if they had used the same form of fighting I used on my brother in the one true fight we had in our younger days.

Kicking your older brother in the groin stops him in his tracks just as fast as a rifle shot, but at least he's still alive, and can drive you to the hospital to have your broken toe X-rayed after you make up.

Section 3
Even I Can Be Serious Every Once in A While

A Canadian 'At Home' In Middle America

I spent a recent weekend in the sort of place that is usually referred to as 'Middle America.' I was in the heartland of Illinois, in a small town called Morris.

As a Canadian, I'm a foreigner in Morris, or anywhere else in the United States for that matter. (I've trouble referring to myself as an alien, especially after all of those movies with Sigourney Weaver.)

Morris is the kind of small town that still has a real downtown shopping district. I'd almost thought places like that had disappeared. The mega-marts are all out near the interstate, but downtown is filled with small businesses.

Morris keeps a lot of moms and pops in business.

It's the kind of place where you see a sign proclaiming *Good Food* and you can be pretty sure there is still truth in advertising in Morris. The fast food places have no toehold in the downtown area. They, too, must cluster out near the interstate; away from the real Morris.

The news on the first morning I spent there contained a story that Illinois residents would not be able to sue fast food restaurants for making them obese. I doubt that anyone in Morris would sue a place advertising *Good Food* for making them obese, even if it did apply a pound or two to their hips.

Places with names like The Liberty Street Café don't make you obese. They make you comfortable.

I was very comfortable in Morris.

The businesses downtown were holding a sidewalk sale the day I was there. Stores had displays out on the street and the citizens of Morris crowded the sidewalks. As I walked down the street, people stopped and said hello. They laughed over some treasure they found in the *everything under a dollar* bin. They smiled at one another.

That kind of behavior is not found in larger cities, and even if you try, you'll soon learn that you are being inappropriate.

I felt appropriate in Morris.

In towns like Morris, hotel rooms don't look out on busy streets. Mine had a view of a cornfield. The corn was as high as the proverbial elephant's eye. The parking lot is next to a field that is vacant, except for a large pond and one old weathered sign, indicating that hunters are not welcome there.

The pond was filled with Canada geese.

Who knew those things could read?

In Morris, homes are made from brick and stone and clean white clapboard. They have pillars and front porches. Flags fly from poles mounted on the front of the houses. Many of the houses are older than I am; older than my parents would be. They have neatly trimmed yards and sit on streets lined with trees that have been there since the houses were new.

They are the kind of houses that would be razed, and replaced with rows of identical condominium townhouses, if they were in a larger city. They may not have three bathrooms or designer kitchens, but they are homes, not just houses. I envy those homeowners.

Some people envy me. They think I lead a glamorous life, traveling throughout North America on my book tours. I get to see cities like Washington, Philadelphia and Los Angeles. These days, it's hard to feel comfortable in those places. One always has it in the back of the mind, that someone might look at those cities as targets.

In Morris, I need only worry about dodging an errant golf ball as I drive along Highway 6.

I was born and raised in Canada. I've lived there for all of my fifty-some years. I'm proud to be a Canadian. That said, Morris reminds me of the lesson I learned on September 11, 2001.

I'm also a North American.

That dark day in September taught me we are all in this together, no matter which side of the forty-ninth parallel we call home. Sitting over a cup of coffee in a town like Morris feels as much like home as if I was sitting in a town like Gravenhurst, Ontario, or Pitt Meadows, British Columbia. Small town Americans and small town Canadians have more things in common than they have differences.

Especially when it comes to a good cup of coffee in the morning.

Stepping Onto My Field of Dreams

It's five o'clock in the morning and I'm sitting in a hotel room in New York. I've been awake for two hours.

I didn't sleep last night. I spent the night getting here, moving from one plane to another, sitting in an airport waiting for my bags to appear, and finally making it to my hotel room.

When you are close to something, even if you don't know how close, or for that matter, exactly what it is, sleep is elusive and almost seems unnecessary.

No, it doesn't just seem that way. I'm beginning to realize that, for whatever reason, sleep is the last thing I need. There is something here I need to experience, and sleep would just get in the way.

In fact, something seems to be at work here to make sure I don't miss the message by doing something as unimportant as sleep. That message seems to be coming at me from a number of sources.

I sat last night with a group of people I don't really know, but then again, I do know them. We all share a common bond. We love the written word, and we work in the business that keeps words in writing, stories in motion, and imagination in everyday life.

We're all in New York for BookExpo-America, the biggest trade show in the business of books. We're authors and publishers, bookbinders and booksellers.

We sat together, with comedian Billy Crystal, talking about his family and his heroes. The stories from his Broadway hit *700 Sundays*. His heroes are the people in his family, past and present. It struck a chord with me, realizing that I too have a lot of heroes, just like his. I thought it was maybe something I should write about.

Back in my hotel room, I fell asleep with the ideas of my personal heroes running through my mind. Sleep came before I had a chance to even get ready for bed. I awoke on top of the covers, in my clothes, my notepad at my side, and the TV still on in the corner.

It was just three o'clock in the morning when I woke up. After just a couple of hours of sleep out of the past forty-eight, I should have been out cold for another several hours, but I didn't just move into a semiconscious state that normally starts the waking process. I snapped into full-fledged, wide awake alertness.

On the TV, a movie had just started. It was *Field of Dreams*. I need to tell you all something about that movie.

A lot of people think it's a movie about baseball and its importance to America.

It's not.

At least, it's not to me.

In the darkest days after the accident that took away so much of what I thought was important in my life, that movie could remind me that dreams can survive adversity.

Whenever I thought my dreams had gone with my ability to walk, I would dig out the tape of that movie, and hope its message was right. I wore out two copies of that tape, and it was one of first I bought when I switched to DVD's.

"If you build it, they will come."

If you dream it, your heroes will help you find it.

On a still-made bed in New York, thousands of miles from home, wearing the clothes I had worn the day before, and after only a couple of hours of sleep out of the past forty-eight, I still got drawn into watching Field of Dreams.

Again.

And then it hit me.

In the movie a ghostly voice was saying, "Go the distance."

I realized that it's your heroes who help you go the distance.

Billy Crystal talked last night about his heroes and how they helped him go the distance, and in doing so, made me think about mine, and what going the distance meant to me. I woke up to a movie about heroes, living your dream, and going the distance.

Maybe it's just a funny coincidence, but it fired a thought through my brain that made it seem like a lot more.

On the TV, Ray Kinsella, the Iowa farmer who built the baseball diamond in an Iowa cornfield, was talking to the ghost of an old country doctor, who, in his youth, had played just one inning in the major leagues. He was a man who had carried a dream of playing baseball with him, even though he had come close enough to just barely touch it.

I'm in New York. I'm at the event that will take me so much closer to the dream I've carried with me for over thirty years. I've come close before, but never this close.

I left high school in 1972 with a dream to be a writer because of a woman named Patricia Cole. Pat taught me English in my senior year, and she planted that dream inside me.

She's one of my heroes.

I've spent my life writing, and for the last eleven, writing a newspaper column, three books (now four) and a whole raft of other articles and stories that give me the title of *Writer*, but I never quite felt like I was in the position to 'go the distance.'

Like the old doctor in the movie, I've had a taste of my dream, but never felt like I was fully touching it.

In the movie, Doctor Cox felt that if just one time, he could stare down a batter, hit the ball and run the bases finally sliding into third, grabbing the bag and hugging it with all his might, he'd really feel like he had grasped a hold of the dream. He'd feel like he had gone the distance.

I'm suddenly being recognized by people who I easily recognize in this business. That's the part of this dream of mine that equates to the old doctor grabbing third base.

A few years after the accident, my wife told me that I should start writing what I wanted write, not the things that other people were hiring me to write for them. She knew that dream was inside me, and had been there throughout our marriage.

Without that push, I wouldn't have started building my personal ball-diamond-in-a-cornfield. I wouldn't have started working on the dream that Pat Cole had planted.

Like the farmer's wife in the movie, she's been the one who had put up with everything that chasing after this dream meant and cost us. She's pushed me on, even when it has not necessarily seemed to be the smart thing to do.

Diane is my consummate hero.

I've an opportunity to feel like I'm grasping a hold of my dream here in New York. I'm in the big leagues of this business here and I've to make sure I last more than just one inning.

I need to go the distance.

I'm being given the opportunity to go the distance.

I'm in my field of dreams.

Maybe, just maybe, if I build it, they will come.

All My Life's A Circle

The late Harry Chapin used to end each concert with the song, *All My Life's A Circle*.

All my life's a circle
Sunrise and sundown
The moon rolls through the nighttime
Til the day break comes around.

That song has been running through my mind a lot this week. I know it doesn't sound particularly like something one would normally think about during the Christmas season. The airwaves are filled with the sounds of Bing Crosby singing *White Christmas* and Mel Torme singing about chestnuts roasting on an open fire. Unfortunately, I will no doubt also be hearing Nana Mouskouri singing *Ave Maria*; something that can just about put me over the edge, but that's another story for another time.

Those songs ringing in the background seems to reemphasize what Harry Chapin was saying.

All my life's a circle, sunrise and sunset.

Each year at this time, we sit and listen to those same songs, decorate a tree, or get a little goofy at an office party, and the circle has come around once again.

I'm writing this column sitting in the airport in Toronto, waiting for a plane to take me home; something I've done so many times before this year. I've sat in the airport waiting to leave, and I've sat in an airport waiting to come home.

All my life's a circle.

Most of my trips this year have been for appearances in different parts of North America. This one isn't. Last Monday morning, my brother-in-law passed away after a heroic fight with cancer.

I flew back to be with my sister through the days leading up to and following the funeral. My sister, brother and I were all together once again, in a city that I had spent so much of my misspent youth. Driving from the Toronto airport to London, Ontario was a route I had taken so many times before. This morning, I reversed the route and returned to the airport.

All my life's a circle.

The funeral was healing. We're an Irish family, so the tradition of the wake the night before was upheld. Bob had requested a plain unfinished casket so that the people at the wake could write messages on it before it went to the crematorium. His grandchildren wrote messages of love, his friends wrote messages and joked with him to the end. One, a master carpenter, wrote, "Nice box, Bob. Why didn't I build it?"

It was hard to say goodbye to a man I had known for over forty years, but all our lives are circles. His just wasn't big enough for my liking.

People are remembered for so many things. Bob Shimer will be remembered for the bright red socks he always wore. I sincerely doubt that he even owned a pair that was white or black or brown.

Whether you were one of the hundreds of students he taught in his career as an elementary school teacher, counselor, and vice-principal, or a camper at Huron Church Camp where he volunteered for nearly thirty years, or part of the legion of friends and family members who are better for knowing him, you'll always think about red socks whenever you think of Bob.

Bob had a sense of style - if you can call it that. The compulsory red socks, together with corduroy pants, a red plaid shirt, and reading glasses perched well down his nose, could be anything from gardening clothes to formal wear in Bob's mind. That image of him was so strong, that the students of the last school he taught in before retiring held a Dress Like Bob Shimer Day, on his final day.

Picture dozens upon dozens of students ranging from kindergarten-age to adolescents, all dressed in red socks, red plaid shirts, corduroy pants, and wearing fake reading glasses they had made from pipe cleaners. It was a fitting way to close the circle that had been Bob's teaching career.

As we said goodbye to Bob at the closing of his casket, we were left with the image of him in his trademark wardrobe. It wouldn't have been right to close that circle any other way.

The last time I talked to Bob on the telephone, he closed off the conversation the same way he had ended every conversation we'd ever had; nothing maudlin or mushy, just a simple, "Bye for now."

Sunset came too early for Bob. People like me are left behind to mourn his passing, and to go on without him. Our circles are still spinning.

All my life's a circle.
And I can't tell you why
The seasons keep on spinning
The years keep rolling by

As if on cue, to further bring home the concept of circles this week, my niece gave birth to a baby boy, just three days after Bob's funeral;and starting a new circle with a new sunrise.

Kyle Robert Bethel, came into the world in time for me to see him before heading back to the West Coast. I got to see one circle close and another begin. Harry Chapin's voice hasn't stopped running around in circles in my mind since I saw the baby yesterday.

During the holiday season we all sometimes feel like we are going in circles. It may even feel like it is out of our control. It puts the words to that song into context with what has gone on in my life over the past seven days, and what is going on in all of our lives as we draw to the end of the circle that is nearing a close on this cold December day,

I can only hope that Harry was right.

All my life's a circle.
Sunrise and sundown
I just can't shake this feeling
That we'll all be together again.

As a new year approaches, to start a new circle, I wish you all happiness, joy, love and peace; the things that Bob Shimer gave to all he knew as they traveled along in his circle.

Bye for now, Bob.

Welcome to the start of your circle Kyle Robert.

All our lives are circles.

Section 4
I Are A Riter... Me Rite Good

A Decade Flies When You're Having Fun

This is the first column in the second decade of *Gordon Kirkland At Large*. The first time it appeared in print was on August 27, 1994 in the Times-Transcript in Moncton, New Brunswick, Canada.

When I started writing the column, my wife and I had been married for twenty-one years. Our sons were fourteen and twelve. My hair had a little bit of gray in it.

A couple of days before the column had its tenth anniversary, Diane and I had our thirty-first. My sons are both quite pleased that their parents' marriage has lasted so long. Their biggest worry in that regard was that, if we ever did split, one of them would end up with custody of me.

The boys grew through their teen years in the column. Looking back over some of those old columns recently, brought back memories of milestones in their lives and the things I had to say about them.

When I look at the promotional pictures that have run with the column over the years I can watch the change that has occurred in my hair color. Despite living with me, Diane's hair hasn't followed suit for some reason.

On teaching one of them to drive: "I have a very important job to do when Diane takes him out to practice driving. I hose down the driveway. That way, when they return, the ground Diane will want to kiss as soon as she gets out of the car will be clean."

On feeding them: "You know you are in trouble when you have run out of food before you finish taking the groceries out of the car."

On driving with them in the car: "The term nuclear family was coined by someone who had inadvertently put two teenage siblings in the backset of the same car. As soon as one touched the other, there was an explosion of nuclear proportions."

Our home was also occupied by another family member through the first seven years of the column. Nipper, the dumbest dog to ever get lost on a single flight of stairs, also provided me with a lot of material.

On occasionally leaving a puddle on the floor: "When Pavlov rang his bell, his dog would drool. Whenever anyone rings our bell, Nipper pees. It's the same concept, just a different end of the dog."

On watching me light the barbeque: "She has a unique vocabulary that she brings out whenever I try to light the barbecue. She runs in circles and loudly yips what, in her canine language, means, 'Oh Geez... He's trying to set fire to the meat again... Don't do it Gord. Let's just eat it raw... You're gonna kill us with that gas barbecue one of these days.' She learned it from my wife."

On her most famous lack of skill: "She gets halfway up the stairs and forgets either where she was going, or how to get there. I often have to come to her rescue when I hear the collection of barks and grunts that clearly mean, "Uhh, Gord... I'm lost again... I'm on that bumpy part of the floor... Every time I take a step there is another bump in the floor in front of me just like the last one... Can I get to my supper dish from here...? Gord... Hey! Gord..."

It's hard to believe that ten years have gone by since I first saw my byline above this column. What started out as something therapeutic for dealing with the changes that took place in my life after my spine was broken and my mobility impaired, has become a regular part of my life. I'm heartened to hear that for many of you, reading it has become a regular part of your lives as well.

Without all of you out there, whether you're a Canadian who has been reading it since the beginning or an American who has seen it for the last few years, there would be no point in sitting down each week and producing these 700 words. Thank you one and all.

I look forward to sharing my take on the humor that surrounds us all every day, throughout the next decade, too.

I Could Write About That, But I Won't

People often ask my why I don't write about politics. There is a perception out there that, if you're going to write humor, politics should be at the top of your topic list.

Not mine.

When I first started in this business, I did write a few politically oriented columns. I quickly learned that people on the fringes don't like people who don't share their opinions. Based on the mail my editors were receiving about me, my political humor was not something that the far left or the far right enjoyed.

My wife started having fears that we would wake up to the sound of a fertilizer bomb going off in our driveway.

One column I wrote got a reaction from both ends of the spectrum. I was called a "typical, West-Coast, liberal, socialist, wacko," by a man whose position seemed to put him just a little to the left of Attila The Hun. Another writer, a man who seemed to spew forth a diatribe against my writing that put him a little further left that Marx, used adjectives like psycho, Nazi, and fascist.

After those letters, I wrote a column titled, *"I Don't Have A Multiple-Personality Disorder... And Neither Do I."*

It made me start to re-evaluate the wisdom of writing political humor. I started to share my wife's fears. I nearly passed out when I looked out the window one day and saw a man unloading bags of fertilizer on the sidewalk at the corner of my property.

Thankfully, it was just the neighbor's lawn care contractor.

So political commentaries were taken off my to-do list, and we both slept easier.

From time to time though, I still get tempted to make the occasional comment about the political events unfolding around us. Let's face it, with both the United States and Canada going through federal election campaigns right now, there is certainly no lack of material.

Politicians are such easy targets. I came to the conclusion long ago that, if a politician's mouth is open, the writers who do risk fertilizer bombs appearing in their driveways, are going to be getting some new material.

Apparently, that's even the case when the mouth is only open for the purpose of eating a pretzel.

But, of course, I would never write about something like that.

Most of us learned to ride a bicycle when we were quite young. It's supposed to be one of those things you never really forget how to do. Apparently, this is not the case for the two men seeking to be the 'leader of the free world' for the next four years. Both candidates for that job had bicycling accidents within days of each other. What does it say about their ability to remember things if neither of them can remember how to ride a bicycle?

These are the guys that American voters want to be able to remember how to cancel a nuclear attack. It's supposed to be as easy to remember as getting back on a bicycle.

But, of course, I would never write about anything like that.

In Canada's election, the right wing is represented by a party that can't decide what to call itself. I've some concerns about people who change their name. What does it say when a political party does it? In the past couple of years, they have called themselves the Conservatives, the Reform, and the Alliance.

...and I was worried about people thinking I might have a multiple personality disorder.

I could quite happily point out in my column that the acronym for the Conservative Reform Alliance Party is CRAP.

But, of course, I would never write about anything like that.

I've always been one who looks for a challenge. In fact, I've often heard people say that I'm challenged.

Writing about political humor is not that much of a challenge - especially when so many politicians also seem to be quite challenged. I could sit at my computer each week and write about politicians who go to extremes to prove to the electorate they are not the sharpest crayons in the box of sixty-four.

But, of course, I would never write about anything like that.

Thanks For Opening The Door For The Rest Of Us, Erma

I'm on the road again.

For the next three and a half weeks I will be traveling through Ohio and Ontario, making appearances in support of my new book. I don't get home until mid-April and then it's only for one day before I head off again for Oregon.

I seem to be getting the places starting with "O" out of the way early.

Part of this tour is something I've been looking forward to for several months. I'm about to be the first Canadian writer on the faculty of the Erma Bombeck Writers' Workshop at the University of Dayton, her alma mater.

I'll be teaming up with a wide variety of humorists to pass along our experience to others wanting to spend their lives writing about the funnier side of life. Others on the faculty include Don Novello, better known as Father Guido Sarducci during his days on Saturday Night Live, Nancy Cartwright, who is the voice of Bart Simpson, Bruce Cameron, the author of the book *Eight Simple Rules For Dating My Teenage Daughter*, and screenwriter Matt Bombeck, Erma's son.

Obviously, it's an honor to have been selected for the faculty of this workshop. Erma Bombeck embodied the role of the humor columnist, and set the standard for so many of us to fall short of.

No other writer in the twentieth century did more to make people see the funny side of everything, from laundry to passport photographs. Every one of us doing this job today owes her a huge debt of gratitude.

My first encounter with her was through her book, *The Grass Is Always Greener Over The Septic Tank*. I can remember seeing that book on a bookstore shelf and immediately knowing that the author knew what she was talking about. Having experienced many a septic tank in my day, I knew just how green and lush the grass could be in that general vicinity. In fact, at our summer cottage, just about the only place that grass would grow at all was over the septic tank.

In the side yard of the first home Diane and I owned, not only was the grass greener around the septic tank, but the ground was a lot squishier, too. Believe me; you never want to have the experience of realizing your feet are sinking into the ground over the septic tank.

I still miss that pair of boots.

Reading her work taught me a lot about how to find the humor in the simple little things that go on all around us. These Bombeck moments have made their way into my columns for the last many years. I've often wondered how she would approach a topic I was writing about. I could almost see her picking up on the same sort of things, especially when one's offspring puts liquid dish detergent for the sink into the dishwasher and then wonders why the kitchen is filling up with bubbles.

Another stop along the way on this part of the tour will also be a bit interesting. When I lived in the town of Maple, Ontario, it was a fair bit north of Toronto.

Today, Toronto has pretty much encircled it.

I lived there from 1960 to 1967 - my elementary school years. In those days, it epitomized the suburbia Erma Bombeck wrote about in her columns and books; unpaved roads, young families, and stay-at-home mothers. Whenever I read her stories, I would picture the streets of similar houses that made up Maple, when she'd be describing her own suburban experiences.

Maple is also where I learned the joy of getting another kid in trouble by making them laugh during quiet reading time. It's also where I learned that you can prevent yourself from getting beaten up if you can get the other guy laughing. On a similar vein I also learned that punishments could be substantially reduced or eliminated if I could make a teacher laugh.

Somehow, it's appropriate I'm doing an appearance in Maple on April First. They're calling the event, *A Fool Returns*.

You probably don't need to wonder why.

You Can't Say That Anymore... Nuts!

It's been roughly forty years since George Carlin talked about the seven words you can't say on television. Anyone who has watched TV in the last couple of years knows that his list has been cut back rather significantly. I doubt that there has been a single episode of *The Sopranos* that hasn't used all seven.

And some of them, repeatedly.

I'm not about to rail against the use of that kind of language in a show like that. Frankly, I find it more of an insult to my intelligence when shows expect we'd hear a mob boss using crystal clean language to describe the person who just shot him.

"Golly gee, Sonny. You've just shot me. You really are a nasty blighter aren't you?"

It just doesn't work, does it?

The Thought Police seem to have pretty much given up trying to stop those seven words from creeping into TV scripts. I half expect to see them as categories on *Jeopardy* one of these days.

"I'll take *Shit* for $800, Alex"

Other words seem to have caught the attention of word banners recently. Most of them are words your grandmother has probably used in the church hall on any given Sunday morning. For that matter I can recall hearing somebody's grandmother using a couple off of George Carlin's list when she dropped a plate of spaghetti at a church supper.

In Nova Scotia, the powers that be have recently issued an edict against certain words in the media. Since my column doesn't appear in a newspaper in Nova Scotia, I can safely tell you what they are. Madman, fruitcake, kooky, nuts, loony, whacko, and bonkers are all forbidden; as are phrases like "lost his marbles."

Frankly, I think the people that came up with this idea are nuts.

Apparently, they feel that these words might offend people who are madmen, crackpots, fruitcakes, kooky, nuts or who may have lost their marbles. Using their thinking, anyone who might wish to say that Saddam Hussein is a madman, should instead say that he is suffering from some form of mental illness.

Since the Canadian one-dollar coin features the likeness of a loon, and is known throughout the land as a loony, I've to wonder about the effect that this rule will have on commerce in Nova Scotia. Will people be limited to using four quarters instead of a single loony?

Before my American readers start thinking it's just those nutty Canadian fruitcakes who are passing edicts like this, I want to remind you that you've had your share of similar rules passed through the legislatures down there too.

Several years ago, Ohio passed a law against saying anything disparaging about vegetables. There are several vegetables that I've often been known to disparage. Broccoli, cauliflower, parsnips, brussels sprouts, and turnip are at the top of my list of vegetables that deserve disparaging at every available opportunity.

And I'm not alone.

George Bush Sr. let his feelings about broccoli be very well known. The loss of the broccoli farmer vote may have cost him his re-election, but he stood firm in his belief that all men deserve the right to life, liberty and saying that broccoli tastes like something the cat coughed up.

The Nova Scotia anti-nutty terminology forces say they are trying to prevent language that might be offensive to people who are suffering from a mental illness. It may be well meaning, but it's still nuttier than a second-hand fruitcake.

The same thing has been tried in an effort to sooth the sensibilities of people like me who have a physical disability. I'd just as soon not be called a cripple, but I'd also rather not be referred to by many of the terms the politically correct language adjusters would like to see used. I'm not sure what is wrong with saying that I've to walk with crutches.

It's sure as heck a lot easier to say than 'mobility disenfranchised.'

I have several words I'd like to use when I write about the people who are wacko enough to think they should be able to tell the rest of us what words to use.

And most of them are on George Carlin's list.

Theeeeerrrrrrrre Goes Johnny!

He may not have been the greatest comedian who ever lived, but there are those who would argue that he was. I will say he did more for comedy than any other person in the twentieth century.

Without Johnny Carson, we probably would never have heard of the likes of Jay Leno, David Letterman, Jerry Seinfeld, or Steve Martin. He gave so many comedians their start. He also rejuvenated the world of comedy for the rest of us.

Anyone making a living in comedy today owes a lot to Johnny Carson.

The Tonight Show was a constant in our home. My parents would drink a strong cup of coffee, eat some cheese and crackers and watch the show. I can often remember waking up in my room across the hall from my parents' to the strains of Carson's theme song – music he wrote together with Paul Anka. I'd strain my ears to try to hear his monologue without my parent's knowledge.

My father worked for General Electric. One night in the early 1960's he brought home a color television set he was taking to a demonstration event the next day. Between my father, brother and me, we managed to get the thing into the house and plugged in. It was definitely not a portable. When we turned it on, we discovered that every show on the air that night was in black and white.

Every show, that is, except *The Tonight Show*.

We all waited, somewhat impatiently, for the show to begin, so that we could see the wonders of color TV.

And what a wonder it was.

Who could have guessed, after only seeing him in black and white, that Johnny Carson would have a bright green face?

My father started twisting knobs on the front of the set. Carson's face turned purple, then back through green to orange. Eventually, he managed to get the face to appear to be somewhat akin to what a Caucasian should look like.

A badly sunburned Caucasian, but at least he was no longer looking like he was about to be physically ill.

I've often thought that Johnny Carson would have gotten a kick out of watching my father trying to adjust the color, while at the same time trying to make us all believe that General Electric was the best television set on the market. Dad was a company man. If General Electric made it, then it was the best and that's all there was to it. We were not even allowed to mention names like Westinghouse, Sylvania, or RCA in his presence.

As the years went by, I saw a lot more of Johnny Carson. Watching him perform was the best education any comedian could ask for. He taught the rest of us how to use timing, how to deal with material that the audience liked, and more importantly, how to deal with the stuff that falls flat.

He could say more just by looking at the camera than many comedians could say in their entire monologues. My most vivid memory of that look came the night the guest with a heavy accent was talking about World War Two German aircraft. Clearly Johnny wasn't prepared for the way he pronounced Fokker.

He taught me a lot of other things, as well. For example:

- Sis-Boom-Baa is the sound of an exploding sheep.
- Take the Slaussen Cutoff, but if you do, be prepared to cut off your slaussen. (I never knew what a slaussen was or where it was, but if I had one, I intended to keep it.)
- No matter how good a comedian you become, you'll still be upstaged by small children and aardvarks with full bladders.
- Never ask a professional golfer's wife if she kisses his balls for good luck.
- Work with people you like, and make sure at least one of them will laugh at everything you say.

The world is going to miss Johnny Carson, even though we've already been missing him since 1992. Thankfully, he left us with so many good memories and countless hours of videotape.

Now that he's gone beautiful downtown Burbank will never seem quite the same.

The Storyteller

A couple of weeks before Christmas, just after my brother-in-law passed away, I wrote a column based on Harry Chapin's song *All My Life's A Circle*. It seemed to be a fitting theme for the feelings I was going through about Bob's passing, the arrival of a new great-nephew, and the impending holiday season.

Shortly after that column appeared, I received a note from Michael Grayeb, who edits *Circle*, a newsletter from the Harry Chapin Archives in Larchment, New York. Michael said that they would like to add the column to the archives and publish it in an upcoming edition of *Circle*.

Over the years, I've received a number of honors and recognitions for my work, but I've to say, this ranks right up near the top. Seeing my picture on the front page of the newsletter may not be quite like what it feels like to be on the cover of *The Rolling Stone*, but it's close enough for me.

Harry Chapin has been gone for over twenty years, the victim of a tragic automobile accident. Most people remember him for songs like *Cats In A Cradle*, *Taxi*, or *W-O-L-D*.

Not me.

I remember Harry Chapin as a storyteller. For me, it was his songs that were too long to make it onto Top-40 radio; the ones that went to great lengths to tell a story without thought or worry about how long it took to get from beginning to end. Whether it was a story about a lonely night watchman from Watertown, New York, an amateur opera singer from Dayton, Ohio, or the poor musician who took the job playing guitar in the dance band on the Titanic, Harry wove a story like few others could ever hope to do.

Thinking about him, one song always seems to come to the forefront of my memories. It was a song about a young truck driver, just out on his second run, who lost control of his rig and died, careening down the hill leading into Scranton, Pennsylvania. The title of the song came from the load he was carrying: *Thirty Thousand Pounds of Bananas*.

If you've ever driven down the hill leading into Scranton, Pennsylvania, try imagining it covered in the remnants of thirty thousand pounds of bananas. Thirty years after I first heard that song, the image still makes me smile.

He used to talk about the importance of hard work. He'd point to the calluses on his fingertips that had built up over time from playing the guitar. While people might have the image that a musician or a writer has a pretty easy job, without the work we put into practicing our craft, we'd never be successful.

I don't have calluses on the ends of my fingers from typing on my keyboard, although my knuckles are starting to feel the affects of the ten-plus years that I've been writing this column. There are even those who would tell you that I've probably got a callus or twenty-two between my ears, but they were probably there long before I started this gig.

Being a storyteller is probably the best job I've ever had. I'm sure Harry Chapin would have said the same thing.

Oh sure, there are weeks when it seems like there is nothing to write about, and I find myself staring at my deadline with a blank computer screen waiting for me to come up with an idea. Still, finding a way to relate the funny side of life I see all around me is as much of a gift to me as it is to anyone who enjoys reading it.

There is one thing that my readers should be thankful for about my stories. I've never thought of putting them into song. Harry took the stories of life he saw and put them into poetic lyrics and added a melody.

It's best that I avoid trying that.

Most of my poetry begins with something along the lines of, "There once was a man from Nantucket…"

And as for my musical ability - let's just say I wouldn't have been picked for the dance band on the Titanic.

I Guess I Shouldn't Be Here

I was feeling pretty good about myself last week, but, as my mother would say, in answer to any question she could not, or would prefer not to, answer, hot air rises and cold air rushes in to take its place.

For years, I thought the facts of life involved turning up the thermostat followed by an influx of cold air. But that's another story.

Last Tuesday I was informed that my second book, *Never Stand Behind A Loaded Horse* (Thistledown), was named one of the five finalists for the Stephen Leacock Award, one of Canada's top book awards. My first book, *Justice Is Blind - And Her Dog Just Peed In My Cornflakes* (Harbour), won the Leacock Award of Merit in 2000.

Sure, it made my head swell. Darn right, it made me feel like hot stuff. I was feeling pretty good right through until Saturday afternoon.

That's when the cold air rushed in to take its place.

I learned on Saturday afternoon that I've been wrong about the way I approached my career as a writer. I should have been better informed about the proper career track for a writer.

In my defense, no one ever told me that I was going astray.

I sat on a panel at a writer's conference on Saturday. I was the lone male on the panel. At one point, I was referred to as 'the trophy man', which I think is somewhat insulting. But the four women on the panel made it clear I was not up to the proper standards necessary to call myself a writer.

One of these learned colleagues laid out the proper career track for the audience. Apparently, the first step is to get accepted into a good MFA program. It took me a moment to translate the acronym into its proper form - Master of Fine Arts.

I had another idea that I think might be more accurate. The first word in my thought was "*Means*", and the last one was "*All*." You can decide for yourself what the second word was, based on its first letter, but I can't say it in a mainstream newspaper column.

Apparently, only by getting into a good MFA program will you learn the proper way to write. That will lead to you getting published, which in turn will lead to the ultimate goal.

...becoming a professor in a good MFA program.

How could I've been so wrong? I never even knew that the goal of every writer was supposed to be to become a professor. I guess it's just my lack of education and drive for career advancement that left me satisfied with being a writer.

Just a writer.

I pointed out the error of my ways to the audience and said I was clearly not qualified to pick up a pen or sit at a keyboard. I attended a university, but learned from one of the greatest poets my country has ever produced that if you want to write you should get out and write.

So I did.

Irving Layton led me astray.

I've spent thirty years writing everything from advertising copy, to strategic plans to responses to letters of complaint sent to Pierre Trudeau when he was Canada's Prime Minister.

That last one gave me my grounding in fiction.

Now I know I should not have been writing, because I had not gotten into a good MFA program first.

Since I started writing this column in 1994, I've written well over five hundred columns, dozens of magazine articles, and four books. I must have neglected to tell the publishers I had not gone to a good MFA program so I had not learned 'the proper way to write.'

All those publishers should have known better than to publish my work.

To make matters worse, in the past year I've been a guest lecturer at Simon Fraser University, The University of Dayton, Florida First Coast Community College, and the University of Georgia.

All without ever having to darken the doors of an MFA program.

So I guess when it comes to being a writer I'm a great big fraud.

Make that an award-winning great big fraud.

It's A Brand New Bouncing Baby Book

Taking a new book from conception to delivery is very similar to taking new offspring from conception to delivery.

When conception of a book occurs there is an immediate rush of excitement, and a feeling of euphoria. With new offspring... well, I rest my case.

After the excitement lapses, fear and questioning of your own abilities start to take hold. Am I ready for this commitment again? Will be able to produce one as good as the last one? At my age, do I've to worry about the risks involved?

All those worries combine to cause a gnawing feeling in the pit of your stomach, which of course leaves you feeling like you are going to be sick at any given moment. I know several authors who have been sick at lots of given moments during the first trimester after signing a publishing contract.

Coming up with a name for a new baby can be an exercise in frustration between what the father might want and what the mother prefers. Believe me, it can be almost the same dealing with a book title. Your publisher has one idea, you have another, and at the last minute the distributor, playing the role of the mother-in-law, makes their desires known.

Bouts of insomnia are not uncommon among expectant mothers and expectant authors. I've always said insomnia wouldn't be so bad if you could just get some sleep while you have it. Expectant authors often lay awake staring at the ceiling thinking about all the work a new book brings with it, just as an expectant mother hashes over all of the responsibilities a new baby brings.

Eventually, a mother will get to see an ultrasound image of her unborn creation. I've tried looking at those pictures in the past, and to the best of my ability, I've always come to the conclusion that the woman is about to give birth to a yak. Authors get to see what are called 'the galleys' of a new book. It is an image of what each page will look like.

Mothers look closely at the ultrasound to see if they can see ten toes and ten fingers and sometimes other more intimate details about their future child. Authors carefully look over every page of the galleys to make sure there aren't any dangling participles or spelling mistakes.

As the due date draws closer, the worries become even greater. Have I done absolutely everything I should have done to make my new creation healthy? Should I've given up drinking while I was waiting for the arrival? For that matter, perhaps if I had given up drinking sooner, this wouldn't be happening to me in the first place.

Mothers and authors watch the calendar during the final trimester. Due dates are circled in red. They both try to bring everything into order so that they are mentally and physically prepared for the arrival.

Of course, due dates are never as precise as we might hope them to be. Our oldest son was four days late. Our youngest was nearly a month overdue. I was beginning to check to see what animals had a ten-month gestation period, because I thought my wife might not be giving birth to a human. The only thing I could find was a two-toed sloth, and I knew that she hadn't been hanging around with any of them.

My first book was overdue. My last one was right on its due date, but the stork dropped it off at the publisher's in a city a thousand miles away from my place, so I had to wait for it to make it's way west.

My new one was early. Having a premature baby causes a lot of stress in parents. The same goes for learning your book is going to come out three weeks earlier than you thought.

"But I'm not ready yet. I haven't had time to prepare everything."

In the end, parents and authors are all pretty satisfied with the results. If we weren't, why would we want to keep doing it?

I'm just glad authors don't have to worry about stretch marks or episiotomy scars.

I Labor (Or Labour) With Spelling

Every couple of weeks, I receive a letter or an email from a reader who is concerned my writing might be leading Canadian youth down the path of sin, depravity, and poor spelling.

The problem arises from my use of the spelling found in Webster's dictionary, instead of the Oxford. I write 'color' instead of 'colour,' and 'neighbor' instead of 'neighbour.'

Sometimes the writers are simply chastising me for my supposed poor spelling. Others feel that I should be dunked in a vat of maple syrup and rolled in feathers from a Canada goose before being left to rot on a beaver dam for being un-Canadian.

I must admit, whenever I type a word like color, I can feel the icy glare of Miss Tilt, my second grade teacher, looking down at me with her twelve-inch ruler slapping against the palm of her hand. It was a look that always clearly expressed that if I did not learn to spell properly, I might start to feel that ruler on the palm of *my* hand, or some other part of my body.

Corporal punishment was all the rage back then.

Of course, by referring to a twelve-inch ruler, I'm leaving myself open to the criticism that I'm also destroying the mathematical abilities of Canadian youth. I should be referring to a 30.48 centimeter ruler. That, in turn, further reinforces my desire to corrupt Canadian youth by not spelling the unit of measure, 'centimetre.'

In my defense, I might point out that in 1961, when Miss Tilt was holding it, it was still a 'twelve-inch' ruler. Canada had not yet switched to the metric system. Therefore, I'm teaching the Canadian youth a history lesson.

There is some spelling that makes me cringe. I see it in common use in both Canada and the United States. Light is not lite. Night is not nite. And the letter c is not completely interchangeable with the letter k.

Hairdressers seem to use that last one a lot. We've all seen places with names like Kutsie Kutters.

Probably the worst example of the misuse of the letter '*k*' came in the last Canadian federal election. There were signs and newspaper ads in my riding that announced a campaign-starting event by Randy Kamp, the candidate for the Conservative Party.

"Kamp's
Kampaign
Kickoff."

Looking at those signs and ads gave me a start. The three capital letters, "KKK," just seemed to be sending the wrong message.

My reason for using Webster's spelling is purely all a matter of numbers.

More newspapers in the United States carry this column than in Canada. Therefore, more Americans read it than Canadians. I'm booked for far more appearances in the United States than in Canada. I'm more likely to be recognized in the United States than on the streets of my own home town, where I'm known simply as Diane Kirkland's husband.

Canadian comedian, Dave Broadfoot, points out that if a Canadian celebrity wants to be recognized he has to wear a nametag.

I've another problem when I go to the United States, though. People there automatically pick up on the Canadian way I say certain words. "Out' and 'about' are the most common ones that give Americans a chuckle. The other, of course, is the habit of ending a sentence with "eh?"

A radio host in Nashville laughed at the way I say the word, "house." He begged me to, "Say it again in Canadian."

I'm proud to be a Canadian. I also have pride in being a North American. There is so much we share and have in common on both sides of the forty-ninth parallel. When we focus on the differences instead of the commonality, we just aren't being neighborly - or neighbourly as the case may be.

It all comes down to one clear underlying fact that is shared by the Canadians who criticize my use of Webster's spelling, and the Americans who laugh at the way I say 'out' or 'about.' If it's me that is writing it or saying it, somebody, somewhere, is going to point out that I'm wrong.

And they may be right.

Section 5
I May Be A Bit Odd, But This Stuff Is Just Plain Strange

Daytime TV Doesn't Cure A Self-Inflicted Headache

I really don't feel like sitting at my computer today. In fact, I really don't feel like doing much of anything.

I'm sick.

My head hurts. My joints hurt. My muscles hurt. Even my brain hurts. Just lifting my head from the pillow took all the energy I could muster. I feel so weak I can barely do the most important thing in a man's life - push the buttons on the TV remote control.

That's what you get for spending an entire weekend at a stag party. A friend of mine's daughter is getting married in a couple of days, and I was invited to the pre-wedding party for the groom. It lasted all weekend, which explains the aforementioned head, joint, muscle and brain aches.

Still, I've managed to learn something today. No one, even if they only have half their normal brain function, should be forced to endure the ravages of daytime TV for more than a couple of consecutive days.

Who came up with the idea to give half the judges in the United States their own TV shows? Is anybody really interested in the outcome of a lawsuit brought before the court by a woman who lent money to her deadbeat neighbor and now expects to be paid?

I realize daytime shows provide a social service. Clearly, Jerry Springer, Montel Williams, Jenny Jones and the rest of the daytime TV talk show hosts, have used up the nation's supply of people who dropped out of school before completing the fifth grade.

There must be a place where old TV shows can go to die. There is barely a timeslot in the day when *M.A.S.H.* isn't showing. The same can be said for *I Love Lucy*. If I ever meet the people who decide to run, and rerun and rerun again the same episodes of *Lucy*, they're gonna have some 'splainin' to do.

If *F-Troop*, *My Mother The Car*, and *My Favorite Martian* have faded into obscurity, we should be able to expect the same fate for *I Dream of Jeanie*, *Bewitched*, and, please God, *The Golden Girls*.

I hate to get started on game shows, but is there any particular reason that *The Price Is Right* still shows up every morning? *Wheel of Fortune* must do a cross-country search for people without enough intelligence to make it on Jerry Springer. Even through my headache and general malaise, I could guess that there wouldn't be a '*W*' in a team name after they had already uncovered "_REEN BA_ PA_KERS."

I've come to the conclusion that the world's biggest example of artificial intelligence is the block of stars on Hollywood Squares.

I refuse to start watching soap operas. On a few occasions, my fingers became too weak to push the remote buttons any further, and I got stuck for a few minutes watching one of these prime examples of overwriting combined with overacting.

I don't know about you, but that certainly isn't what the days of my life looks like.

Even the sports channels are a major disappointment during the day. My body already feels like I've been at the bottom of a pile-up of WWF wrestlers. I don't really want to watch grown men pretending to fight in their underwear.

I've no interest in the outcome of a field hockey game between two countries I can't even pronounce.

My head hurts even more when I watch a guy return a trophy-size trout to the water after spending an hour reeling it in. I think it's an extension of my subconscious mind letting me know what it would be like to get hit in the head with a boat oar, because that is what would have to happen to get me to send the fish back.

There is one good thing about the level of quality found on daytime TV: It's giving me the willpower to get better as soon as possible. Even though I feel like something the dog left in the long grass in the field at the end of my street, if I have to watch another episode of Gilligan's Island I might do something rash.

Like get up and work.

Warning: Columnist Under Pressure

Warning: This column is not fireproof. It should not be substituted for a personal floatation device, and, perhaps most importantly, should not be used internally.

While it doesn't contain nuts, it was written by someone a lot of readers think just might be nuts, therefore those with allergies should be forewarned.

Just about everything we buy these days comes with some sort of warning label. Often, when I read these labels, I have to wonder if the manufacturers of the products think I'm crazy.

It's probably not me they are worried about, but the only good reason I can see for my wife's curling iron to come with the warning that it should not be used internally, is because someone, somewhere, once tried to curl something they shouldn't have.

Just thinking about that is wrong on so many different levels.

The real reason these warnings have proliferated faster than rabbits on Viagra™, is because the manufacturers do not want to be sued for someone's third degree rectal burns. It all started when someone sued a restaurant because the coffee they spilled on themselves was hot.

Well, duh!

I still can't understand how someone's clumsiness with a cup of coffee can result in a lawsuit against the restaurant who served it to them. But it did. Now whenever we stop at a drive-through for a coffee, the cup comes complete with a warning label saying, "Caution: Contents May Be Hot."

I certainly hope so.

An organization called the Michigan Lawsuit Abuse Watch recently held a contest for the strangest warning label on a consumer product. The winner of the $500 first prize sent in a toilet brush with the brush attachment designed to be disposed of after each use that bore a warning we all should obey.

"Do not use for personal hygiene."

I can only imagine what would go through someone's mind to make them do that.

"Well, I can't find my luffa, so I guess I'm just going to have to scrub with the toilet brush,"

"...again."

Second prize went to someone who sent in the label from a child's scooter.

"This product moves when used."

Someone must have bought one and said, "Come here Johnny. Look what your daddy bought you. It's a scooter you can just stand on to watch TV. Here try it out. Oh my Lord, it's moving. Somebody save my child!"

The third prize of $100 went to the person who submitted a digital thermometer with the warning, "Once used rectally this thermometer should not be used orally."

"But Mommy, the thermometer tastes funny..."

When English is not the first language of the company making a product the warnings can get a little odd. I have a plastic bag I kept after opening a new coffeepot. The warning on the bag says, "Keep away from children and pens."

It's been in my desk drawer for several years, and it doesn't seem to have had any adverse affects on my ballpoints.

It's also been widely reported that a Korean-made knife comes with the warning, "Keep out of children."

Lately, when packages arrive in my office, many of them contain small bags full of air instead of the Styrofoam packing peanuts that my cat likes to eat. These things are not large. Most are about three inches by less than ten inches, but they are clearly marked that they should not be used as a personal floatation device.

"Timmy fell in the lake. Quick someone throw him a packaging pillow."

Some of the past winners of the Michigan Lawsuit Abuse Watch competition include:

- A label on a baby-stroller warning: "Remove child before folding."
- Purchasers of a brass fishing lure with a three-pronged hook on the end are warned: "Harmful if swallowed."
- And perhaps my personal favorite, a warning on an electric drill made for carpenters points out: "This product not intended for use as a dental drill."

"You say you've got a toothache, George? Wait right here. I'll go home and get my drill."

Of course, the biggest warning sign of them all is on Interstate 20:

"You are now entering Alabama."

Attention! Attention!

Anyone who has spent any time in New York will tell you it is a place to see the strange and the unusual without having to buy a ticket for the show.

It's apparent some people will do just about anything to be noticed. While they succeed in that particular goal, they don't seem to realize they are not getting noticed for reasons that will do them much good.

I spent last weekend in New York at BookExpo-America, the largest industry trade show for the publishing business. Publishers, booksellers, authors, and companies providing services to the other three groups, all gathered for a collective experience of work, play, and things that can't be written about in a mainstream newspaper.

I, of course, was a good boy and didn't take part in any of the latter activities, with the exception of the drinking. Even that wasn't so bad, other than the fact I'm not entirely sure how I got back to my hotel room on Saturday night.

I guess I should just consider it a good thing I did wake up there on Sunday morning.

The trade show was filled with celebrities, near celebrities, and some who are in an entirely different universe from being, or becoming, a celebrity. Those were the ones who caught my attention, probably because they went out of their way to make themselves noticed, and even through hung-over eyes, they stood out like broccoli on a table of good-tasting food.

One man wanted the world to know he had written a book that had something to do with toilets. He wandered the show floor wearing a toilet seat around his neck with the lid tied to the back of his head. His book title was scrawled on the inside of the lid in what I hope was ink. Around his neck, beneath the seat, was what looked like a scorched roll of toilet tissue.

Oh, he was noticed all right.

Most people gave him a lot of extra room in the aisles.

I know I will probably get into trouble with a certain percentage of my readers if I comment on one of the sillier ways some people of a certain gender chose to draw attention to themselves. These people make a statement by wearing a particular piece of clothing to excess.

Women's hats.

I'm not talking about simple little hats like pillboxes, ball caps, or even Stetsons. Some women seem to have a need to let the world know they are approaching several minutes before they actually arrive, by wearing hats that would fit on the Statue of Liberty.

One particular woman wore a black hat that had to be at least three feet across. The brim held a collection of plastic fruit.

She looked like a walking buffet table.

Of course, the show was filled with walking versions of characters from books. There was the Pink Panther, Big Bird from *Sesame Street*, several *Star Wars* characters, and a lot that I failed to recognize.

These poor people had to don heavy costumes that turned into miniature saunas as they wandered around the trade show floor.

You could always tell how long the person had been wearing the suit by their posture and actions. When they first put the suit on, they would walk tall, waving to everyone in the crowd. After about twenty minutes their backs were curved, their arms hung limply at their sides and they walked with all the enthusiasm of a prisoner-of-war.

My publisher's booth was home to something called the Schmooney. It's from a children's book about an animal that is made up of parts of several others, including a rabbit's ears, a beaver's tail, a raccoon's head, and more. After wearing the suit for a half an hour, the staff members assigned to the task looked like they had run a marathon.

And not well.

I prefer a more subtle form of attracting attention to my books. Seeing a book with a title like, *When My Mind Wanders It Brings Back Souvenirs* will stick in someone's mind on its own, and I don't have to wear a funny hat.

Or a toilet seat.

Ready... Aim...

It's been five years since the world breathed a collective sigh of relief, that the gloom and doom predictions about what would happen when we entered the new millennium didn't happen. Of course, now that I've said that, I will undoubtedly get a couple of letters from anally-retentive people who insist that the new millennium didn't start until January first, 2001.

If you'll recall, the catchphrase of the day was, "Y2K."

All sorts of disasters were supposed to befall us as the calendars switched from '99 to '00. Computers were going to malfunction, planes were going to drop from the sky, communications would be disrupted, and an epidemic of severe constipation was due to be unleashed.

Of course, none of that happened and we sailed through the date change unscathed. I do, however, still have a supply of laxatives that should last me until the next impending disaster is predicted.

Technology has kept advancing over the past five years. Some of those advances are quite obvious. The computer I use today is a laptop that has the equivalent power of twenty of the large desktop computers like the one I was using in 2000.

Other advances are not so easily spotted, and it is my duty as a newspaper columnist to try to keep my readers informed of the technology improvements that are going to change the way they do their business in the future.

A news item crossed my desk last week about one such advance. Doing your business may never be the same, now that the Wizmark interactive urinal communicator has arrived.

According to the manufacturer's website, "Wizmark is based on one unwritten rule of men's room etiquette; when using a urinal, never stare at the person next to you. Every male knows that when he is using a urinal, he can look anyway he wants, except left or right. Realizing this unwritten code, the appeal of this marketing concept to you as an advertiser is that it effectively assures your ad will attract the attention of, and be read by, the ever elusive targeted male audience you are constantly aiming for. Wizmark's interactive capabilities will get results, providing the perfect guerilla marketing medium for men of all ages."

It goes on to say, "As a one-of-a-kind, fully functional interactive device, Wizmark can talk, sing, or flash a string of lights around a promotional message when greeting a "visitor". The large anti-glare, water-proof viewing screen is strategically located just above the drain to ensure guaranteed viewing without interruptions. Using the elements of surprise and humor in a truly unique location will allow Wizmark, in combination with your ad, to make a lasting impression on every male that sees it."

If a urinal suddenly started flashing lights and talking to me, I think it would undoubtedly make a lasting impression on my pant leg.

In the example message cited in the news article I read about this development, a female voice says, "Don't miss *Outlaws* on CMT. You seem to miss everything else."

Well, of course, the poor guy who triggered the device is having trouble with his aim. Hearing a female voice coming from the bottom of the urinal would probably be enough to cause many men to miss the target, although the ceiling, walls, and cologne dispensing machine might all become targets.

At least they won't talk back.

I can only imagine the messages that might come from Wizmarks around the nation. (You all knew that was going to happen, didn't you?)

"Hey, that's not very much. Maybe you should get a prostrate exam."

"What the heck have you been drinking? Dishwashing detergent?"

"Aaaaaargh! My eyes! My eyes!"

"...and you think you have a lousy job."

"Hey! You! I'm talking to you, Buster. You forgot to flush last time you were in here."

The development of the Wizmark ranks right up there with the toilet seat that doubles as a bidet. Both of them scare the heck out of me. The last thing I want to be worried about when I really have to go, is the possibility of a short circuit, especially when I remember the sight of one of my past dogs after it peed on an electric fence.

I don't think I could somersault like that anymore.

A New Upstanding Female Activity

While it might come as a surprise to many women, I'm reasonably liberated regarding feminist issues. I'm even secure enough in my manhood to admit that.

If you ask my wife, she will tell you that I've always supported her in her career ambitions, and have been a firm believer in equal pay for equal work. If a woman wants to slop hogs, she should expect to receive the same pay as a male hog slopper.

I also believe that a woman can perform the duties of any job just as well as her male counterpart. In many cases, women can do much better than men, even in roles that have traditionally been male bastions in the workplace. My wife has often been the first woman in the jobs she's held.

Over the past thirty years or so, we have seen so many male-dominated areas fall. Men's clubs, men-only golf courses, and men's boxer shorts as a female fashion statement, are just the tip of the iceberg.

There was one thing I thought would always be something that was just for men, and women would never know the experience, to say nothing of the convenience it offers us.

But all things must pass, and in this case, all things must pass water.

The ability to pee standing up is no longer a male-only preoccupation.

A Dutch invention called P-Mates, has come to the rescue of women who want the experience of peeing in an upright position.

According to the Canadian distributor's website, the product is made from recycled paper that has been turned into a waxed cardboard. It is quick, clean, leak-proof and it folds to fit into a pocket or a purse.

I found the instructions for using it slightly deficient, but I can chalk that up to female inexperience with peeing while standing. They gave a four step process for using the product:

1. Simply pop open the P-mate and move your panties aside and place the cupped area under the flow area between your legs.
2. Have the funnel facing slightly downwards.
3. Relax and pee.
4. Dispose of the used P-Mate in the garbage.

Any man will tell you that they neglected a very important fifth instruction. As the product is primarily designed for use while hiking or taking part in some other outdoor activity, users not accustomed to the practice should be reminded to always face downwind.

I can recall a situation in which a P-Mate might have kept me out of trouble. We had driven deep into the mountains in the late fall, along a quiet country road. After an hour or two, Diane announced that her liquid intake had exceeded her liquid storage capabilities. There were no gas stations, restaurants, or even houses along the road where we might have stopped.

Finally, we came to a state park.

It was deserted. We found some outhouses but they had been locked up for the season. Diane resigned herself to trudging off into the woods to find a hiding place, in case some other bladder-filled driver came by.

She didn't seem to appreciate me honking the horn and waving wildly at her while she hid in the bushes a couple of hundred yards away from the park road. I was quite impressed to discover that she had such incredibly good balance that she was able to take care of the business at hand, and still lift one finger up to wave back at me.

I continued honking and waving, but she didn't seem to appreciate the message I was trying to transmit. She stormed back to the car and let me know just how she felt about having me call attention to her in that precarious position.

"Dear," I said, "I wasn't calling attention to you. I was trying to call your attention to that cave you had your back to. It looks like it's home to either a black bear a cougar."

I would have thought she might have appreciated my concern for her wellbeing, but apparently, if a woman pees in the forest a husband shouldn't make a sound.

Words to live by...

Oh Look, Buddha In My Bratwurst

It's no secret I like food.

I've always liked food. As a result I grew up having my clothes purchased in the '*husky boys*' department, and to this day, must shop for my clothes in stores with names like Mr. Humungous.

There are items some people think are food that I refrain from eating. I will not let broccoli pass my lips - but then, broccoli isn't really food. It, along with turnip, parsnips, Brussels sprouts, and cyanide, all fit within the category of noxious substances.

I had a teetotaling relative who would say, "Lips that touch liquor shall not touch mine."

Beside making me develop a taste for alcohol by the time I was eight to avoid having to kiss her when she'd visit, it did leave me with the thought that one could be selective about who one might feel comfortable kissing.

Therefore, lips that touch cauliflower shall not touch mine.

We have such a wide selection of foodstuff available today, I think it is just fine to be somewhat selective in what we will or will not willingly put in our mouths.

Cucumbers, yes. Artichokes, no.

And that's a big, big no.

Basically, I know what I like and I like what I know. I know that carrots, peas, beans, tomatoes, lettuce, celery, and asparagus taste good. Leave me with those, and don't try to introduce me to tofu.

I like to be able to sit down to a meal or a snack and eat it. I don't want to have to examine the meal to see if someone has tried to hide broccoli in the spaghetti sauce. I also don't want to have to examine every bite to make sure I'm not eating something bearing the abstract image of Jesus, the Virgin Mary, Mother Theresa, or Marvin the Martian.

Hardly a week goes by lately without someone finding Jesus. I don't mean that they have suddenly made a religious conversion. I'm talking about the people who find Jesus in a scorched image on a potato chip, piece of toast, or staring out from the air bubbles in an ice cube.

There seems to be a common theme from all of the people who find this sort of religious icon in their snack food. It has nothing to do with piety.

"Gee," they think, "I wonder what I can get for this on eBay."

There is a company buying up these items, largely for the publicity it gives them. That's why I'm not going to bother mentioning their name. People are getting thousands of dollars for things like grilled cheese sandwiches and pretzels, that, if you really use your imagination, might show you the face of a religious figure.

On the other hand, they might also show you the image of a puppy, a choo-choo, or a pussy.

The latest potato chip shown on network television that supposedly bears the image of Jesus, takes a bit of imagination. When I looked at it I wasn't sure. Oh yes, there were two eyes and a beard that were fairly easy to spot, but was it Jesus or a young Fidel Castro?

The effect, of course, is that people are examining every piece of food that they eat, just in case they see Moses in their Kosher dill pickle, Jesus in their bagel, or Mary in a cheese Danish. With my luck, I'd only find Job, complete with all of his sores, staring up from a cinnamon bun.

I'm not absolutely certain, but it will take an awful lot to convince me there is not the image of Satan hiding somewhere inside every turnip. I also believe that every broccoli sprig is an exact replica of a tree growing somewhere around the seventh ring of hell.

Perhaps I'm just jealous. I'm not the one getting ten thousand dollars for a piece of toast with a fuzzy human form that could - or could not - be identified as a religious figure. I know it is very unlikely I will ever see an image of Jesus on a tortilla chip.

Of course, that's because it wouldn't be visible through the guacamole and salsa.

This Spam Doesn't Go With Eggs And Toast

It's getting so I hardly want to open my email program anymore. As I look down the list of new messages, I feel like I'm in the chorus of Eric Idle's Tony Award-winning musical *Monty Python's Spamalot*.

"Spam... spam... spam... spam..."

I get a few messages from friends, colleagues, and readers who want to point out how much of an idiot they think I'm this week, and dozens upon dozens of messages suggesting I buy something, win something, or do something to my body.

I'm flooded with offers for replica watches. I have a replica watch that I bought in Thailand sixteen years ago. It cost me the equivalent of about five dollars, not the few hundred these email watch dealers want for the same thing.

Even if I returned to Thailand, I wouldn't pay five bucks for another one of those watches, because it barely kept time and it made my wrist turn green.

I have to chuckle at the ones that come in offering to sell me cheaper Canadian medications. They offer all the popular drugs like Viagra or Cialis, and, just in case I feel a little blue about the cost of my medications, they'll even ship me cheap Canadian Prozac, Xanax, Valium, and Paxil.

Hello...? Remember...? I'm a Canadian.

I can already get cheap Prozac at the drug store down the street.

I also get a lot of emails about drugs that are supposed to work just like a name brand drug but at a reduced price. If a fake Rolex can turn my wrist green, I'd hate to think what fake Viagra might do.

Two junk emails that arrive at least once a day seem to contradict one another. One offers me up to $400,000 for as little as $350.00 a month. The second suggests that its sender can help me eliminate all my debt without paying it off. Somehow, I think if I used both their services, someone looking like Tony Soprano -

representing the lender - would show up at my door with a baseball bat for my knees.

Every day or so, I get an email from the United Kingdom offering to sell me a product that will make me more attractive to women by dousing myself with pheromones. I guess it might be useful in England. After all, it won't be their mastery of the culinary arts that makes them attractive to women. I should think it would take a whole bottle of liquid pheromones to offset the reaction they might get for offering to cook a woman a lovely meal of mad cow entrails and blood pudding with chips.

I can always count on receiving a batch of emails offering to send me pornographic photographs and videos. They're wasting their time. I don't look at that kind of thing anymore. My mother told me I'd go blind if I looked at them, and I've kept my promise I'd quit as soon as I needed glasses.

OK, so I have to wear trifocals. What's your point?

I also get a lot of emails offering to sell me a product guaranteed to make a certain part of my body grow substantially. The product comes in a patch, like the kind people wear who are trying to quit smoking. When you consider what it is supposed to do, and what part of the body it's supposed to do it to, I get uncomfortable just thinking about how much it would hurt trying to take the thing off.

That's not the only thing that makes me an unlikely customer for that product. As most of you already know, I've to walk with crutches as it is. I'm very good at falling over. In the past fifteen years since the accident that left me this way, I've a perfect record. I've managed to hit the ground each and every time, and in doing so, I think I've broken each of my ribs at least once.

If this product does what the emails claim, it sounds like it would completely throw off what's left of my center of balance.

Give Me The News, Not The Reality

I have a TV in my office that tends to be left on during the day. I start the day with the morning news and by the time it's over, I'm already working and can't be bothered to get up and turn it off.

I'd keep the remote on my desk, but after the first few minutes it would be buried under papers and other assorted stuff, and it might never be seen again.

The morning news show I watch gives me everything I need to know about what's going on in the world and interesting interviews, all wrapped up in an entertaining package that is fun to watch.

I want a nice concise newscast. There are certain facts I need to know before starting my day. Did North Korea launch a missile attack on my small semi-rural community? Is there even the slightest chance that the National Hockey League will be playing again this year? Are there any reports of my death?

These are important things to know before starting work.

If North Korea did decide to launch an attack on sub-suburban Vancouver, I'd want to have enough time to practice that drill we were taught in school in the Fifties.

I'm just not sure I can still fit under my desk.

It's critical that the National Hockey League plays again this season, My American readers might not all understand the significance, but here in Canada, we need hockey. It's our one chance to let out our repressed violence. If hockey doesn't come back soon you're going to start seeing Canadians joining the NRA, attacking countries that have even smaller military forces than ours (Greenland comes to mind), and forgetting to excuse ourselves if we sneeze.

Oh the humanity...

Obviously, it's important that I get confirmation I'm still alive. I'd hate to think I was spending my afterlife sitting at my desk.

The other reason I watch this particular newscast is that they are one of the few media organizations in my home area who actually know who I am, and what I do for a living. Despite all the success I've had writing this column for the past eleven years, it has never, in all that time, appeared in a newspaper in this area. Since they invite me to join them on the show from time to time, I think it's probably the least I could do to watch them every morning.

During the rest of the day, the TV just provides background noise in the office. Who knows? Perhaps I could subliminally learn how to cook a Thai-Kosher-fusion chicken cacciatore from the cooking show that follows the news. I might find out how to redecorate the linen closet from another one of the shows. I might even get useful ideas about how to reorganize my office, my wardrobe, and my physique.

Yeah, right. I don't believe that either, but the TV station keeps trying to tell me I can do it.

There is one show that can send me rushing to find the remote to get the TV turned off as quickly as possible. A couple times a week, the station dedicates a half hour to a bit of reality programming that has fewer redeeming qualities than an infomercial.

They've set up TV cameras in stores and other public areas around the city where people can deposit a bit of cash and get their own moment on TV. Oh sure, the money goes to charity and that's a good thing, but the tape goes to air and that's a bad thing.

A very, very bad thing...

Just as furniture salesmen and car dealers should be legally prevented from making their own commercials, drunken wedding shower guests, amateur country, hip-hop, or pre-teen singers, stoned political commentators, and especially the guy who steals, and then messes up the telling of comedians' material, should all be precluded from buying TV time for a buck.

I have to admit, the woman who stands in front of the camera hitting it because she thinks it took her money without turning on the camera is funny stuff.

I just wish she'd hit the camera a whole lot harder.

.

About the Author

Gordon Kirkland was born in Toronto, Ontario, Canada in 1953. He met his wife, Diane, while still in high school in London, Ontario. Married in 1973, they've spent over thirty years as each other's best friend. They have two grown sons, Mike and Brad.

Since 1982, they've lived on Canada's West Coast in a small semi-rural community near Vancouver, British Columbia.

Gordon became partially paralyzed in a 1990 automobile accident. He jokes that it was really a golfing accident, because he was on his way to play golf when his car was rear-ended. In 1992, he was once again hit from behind by an errant driver. When it happened again in 1994, this time by a member of the Royal Canadian Mounted Police, he began to think that even numbered years in the 1990's were out to get him.

He was almost afraid to drive in 1996.

He spent his working life writing in a variety of functions ranging from public relations and advertising to marketing and strategic planning. Immediately prior to his first accident, he wrote six books for the Government of Canada focusing on trade opportunities in countries in Southeast Asia.

Diane encouraged him to start writing the way he would like to, rather than writing what other people wanted him to write for them. He chose to focus on humor, partially because of his upbringing in a family that included a great deal of laughter, and because, during his hospital rehabilitation after the accidents, he learned that laughter causes the body to produce endorphins that are ten times stronger than morphine.

As he says, "...and I was so enjoying the morphine."

The result has been his three previous books and the book you are now holding.

His first, Justice *Is Blind - And Her Dog Just Peed In My Cornflakes*, won Canada's Stephen Leacock Award of Merit for Humour in 2000. His second, *Never Stand Behind A Loaded Horse*, won the same award in 2005. Following the trend, his third book, *When My Mind Wanders It brings Back Souvenirs*, won him his third Award of Merit in 2006 .

In addition to his books, his weekly syndicated humor column, Gordon Kirkland At Large, has appeared in Canadian and American newspapers since August, 1994. In that time he has written hundreds of newspaper columns and feature articles, a live comedy CD, a live audio book, and four volumes of contact management information for writers.

Gordon's life and humor have been profiled in magazines and newspapers throughout North America. He has appeared on dozens of radio and television talk shows, as well performing his material as in theaters and comedy venues.

Each year, he makes himself available to writer's conferences, festivals and workshops, where he teaches a wide variety of topics ranging from humor writing to book marketing. Most notably, he has been a member of the faculty of the prestigious *Erma Bombeck Writers' Workshop* at the University of Dayton in Ohio since 1994.

His outlook on life, which shines through in his writing, makes him living proff that adversity and life's difficult events can be handled successfully as long as you maintain your sense of humor.

Printed in the United States
69247LVS00006B/52-123

9 781425 914059